VOLUME
FOUR THOUGHTS
FOR ONE
HUNDRED DAYS

VOLUME FOUR THOUGHTS FOR ONE HUNDRED DAYS

Selected from

*"Thought for the day" and
"the spoken word" as heard
on radio and television*

by

Richard L. Evans

PUBLISHERS PRESS
Salt Lake City, Utah

VOLUME IV

THOUGHTS FOR 100 DAYS

Copyright © 1970 Atesons

Printed in the United States of America

For information address Publishers Press

1900 West 2300 South, Salt Lake City, Utah 84119

FIRST EDITION

3rd Printing, 1971

LITHOGRAPHED IN U.S.A. BY

PUBLISHERS PRESS
SALT LAKE CITY, UTAH

Contents

PART 1

"Now's the day and now's the hour."

—Robert Burns

"... *that is all there is to you* ..."

There is a line from Emerson which somewhat summarizes life's purpose in one short sentence: "Make the most of yourself," he said, "for that is all there is to you."[1]

Each man is always and forever inseparably himself. Each one of us is always with himself. We are constantly in our own company. We are a combination of mind, of spirit, of physical faculties, which we use, or fail to use, in one way or another. Either we learn — or we don't know; either we practice — or we don't improve. Either we commit ourselves to the wholesome opportunities of life — or we slip to something less than we could have become.

We build the record of what we are; we build the very substance of ourselves by the choices and decisions of every hour, of each instant. We can become much more, or we can become much less, but we never get away from ourselves.

Sometimes young people drift along in school, in work, or in not much of anything at all, thinking they don't need to put out much effort — just getting by, just loafing along, doing as little as possible. While this may be disappointing to others, ultimately it is damaging principally to one person — to him who doesn't learn and work and produce and prepare himself. As Emerson said it, ultimately and actually, "It is impossible for a man to be cheated by anyone but himself."[2]

Who would be so shortsighted as to be indifferent to the opportunity to learn — or to take the low road, or choose to break the law — so shortsighted as to partake of things that would lower the morals, or injure the body or mind or spirit of any man.

Life is forever, and the pursuit of excellence must be forever: learning, developing, making ourselves more serviceable, living so as to have a clear, quiet conscience, in cleanliness, in honor, in health, in happiness — becoming the best we can become, with reverence and respect.

"Make the most of yourself, for that is all there is to you." To do less would be foolishly, stupidly shortsighted.

"If I am not happy with me"

From a thoughtful observer of human behavior, this sentence seems significant: "If I am not happy with me, other people suffer."[3] Our attitudes and actions toward others often depend more upon how *we* feel than upon what *they* do. When we are tired or troubled we may react impatiently, critically; but when we are relaxed and untroubled we react quite differently to precisely the same situation.

What we feel inside, what we know concerning ourselves, often determines our reaction to others. For example, people are not likely to be pleasant when they have a sense of guilt, when they are fighting themselves inside.

Sometimes young people decide to rebel, to disobey, to live contrary to counsel, and when they do they begin to fight themselves, and so become unpleasant and unhappy wherever they are. This reminds us of a simple sentence from Abraham Lincoln: "When I do good I feel good, and when I don't do good I don't feel good."[4] With all of us, it is just that simple. We may say, as Shakespeare said it, "The time is out of joint"[5] when it may be we who are out of joint.

If we are studying well, doing well, meeting our obligations, seeing people without a sense of apology, we are pleasant with people. On the other hand, we tend to dislike those whom we have wronged or mistreated because we dislike ourselves for doing it — and when we dislike ourselves, we dislike others also. It is bad enough to suffer for our own mistakes, but worse to make others suffer for things *they* didn't do.

The remedy is to live in honor and cleanliness and kindness so we can avoid accusing ourselves and quarreling with conscience. "When I do good I feel good, and when I don't do good I don't feel good." "If I am not happy with me, other people suffer."

On being bored

Young or old, one of the most down-pulling attitudes in life is being bored. Sometimes we become bored with routine, with what we feel are repetitious and unchallenging tasks. But there is repetition and routine in all assignments, in all activities and occupations.

Teachers have hundreds of lessons to teach. Artists practice over and over again before performing. Doctors have patients to see and symptoms to listen to, countless repetitious times. Those who make things, those who do things, those who direct others to do things, do them over and over again. And so it is, from the least responsible to the most responsible position.

Perhaps no one knows better than wives and mothers about repetition and routine — with thousands of dishes to be washed; with clothes, over and over again, to be cleaned and tended to; meals to be cooked time after time — and unnumbered other chores unnumbered repetitious times. But drudgery and boredom are relieved by love and appreciation, and by a sense of service.

Even the work of God, it would seem, must be repetitious, because life is renewed, commandments repeated, and the seasons follow in succession. Sunrise is repetitious — and springtime, and so are all seasons.

Life, fortunately, is repetitious. And there can be satisfaction in the simplest assignment, and there can be boredom in the most exciting assignment — depending on the inner attitude.

Despite all repetition and routine, every new day is a miracle, an opportunity, and every essential service is its own reason for living every day of life. Every unknown truth is an endless invitation. Even if we are confined physically, our minds can range widely over the earth.

"Life is always opening new and unexpected things for us," wrote Phillip Brooks. "There is no monotony in living to him who walks . . . with open and perceptive eyes. The monotony of life, if life is monotonous to you, is in you, not in the world."[6]

Do your work; meet life as it is, know that each service is essential — and never be bored.

"And that has made all the difference"

In looking back we often see where we took one way instead of another — where we might have done differently. This, in one sense, is what happened to Scrooge in Dicken's Christmas Carol. He saw where and what he would be *if* he continued his present course.

But we don't need to be taken on tour by an unearthly messenger, as Scrooge was, to see, in some respects, the same thing. There is all the experience of the past, the laws, the principles, the wisdom of the ages, the commandments of God. There is all of history which has proved and disproved many things. And regardless of cynical thinking and pandering to undisciplined appetites and inclinations, seeking to set aside the laws of life is finally fruitless — for in a very real sense the laws of health, the moral laws, the basic laws of life are self-enforcing.

If we want to arrive at a place of peace and self-respect, of competence and accomplishment, we can choose the road in the same sense as a traveler decides where he wants to go, and looks at the map and follows the signs to get there. He is going to arrive at where the road he is traveling takes him. If he is traveling the wrong road he is going to arrive at the wrong place, unless he changes direction.

We have life to live. We have a choice of many ways to live it. Whether it is education, competence, family, friends, respect, peace — whatever it is we want — we had better study the route, we had better learn the rules. Peace and happiness don't come by rebelliously traveling the wrong road. This from Robert Frost seems to summarize the subject:

> I shall be telling this with a sigh
> Somewhere ages and ages hence:
> Two roads diverged in a wood, and I —
> I took the one less traveled by,
> And that has made all the difference.[7]

You . . . grown older . . .

There is an old man up there ahead of you that you ought to know. He looks somewhat like you, talks like you, walks like you. He has your nose, your eyes, your chin: and whether he loves you or hates you, respects you or despises you, whether he is angry or comfortable, whether he is miserable or happy, depends on you. For *you* made him. He is *you*, grown older."[8]

This has both caution and promise depending upon which direction we choose to take. "We live forward, we understand backwards,"[9] said

William James. And yet we are not altogether at a loss to know, along broad lines, where any road will lead. There are many who have traveled almost every road that we might choose to take; there are many who have done most things that we might choose to do, and we can look to the principles that have been proved and the results that have been realized in the lives that others have lived.

Every young person, for example, can know that patience, preparation, learning, working are essential for a fullness of life. Any observer, of the present or the past, may know that cleanliness of body, of mind and morals is kindly and peacefully comfortable; that uncleanliness is coarsening and corrosive; that standards are essential; that personal responsibility is real; that law sustains life: that there are consequences for every act; that "wickedness never was happiness;"[10] that the commandments are founded on eternal facts.

If we live one way we get one result — if we live another way we get another result. We ought to be smart enough, realistic enough, observant and alert enough to know this, forward as well as backwards.

"There is an old man up there ahead of you that you ought to know . . . Whether he is miserable or happy, depends on you. For *you* made him. He is *you*, grown older."

"To be what we are, and to become what we are capable of becoming, is the only end of life."

—Robert Louis Stevenson

PART 2

"He that is taught only by himself has a fool for a master."

—BEN JONSON

The "get-out-from-under" attitude . . .

There is sometimes evident an attitude of wanting to get out from under, not wanting to be accountable to anyone. Young people, for example, sometimes choose to move away from home and family and friends. Work, education, opportunities in other areas, are often good reasons.

But to leave just to cut loose, just to go it alone, just to be free from being accountable to anyone may well not be wise. And before we feel we want to get away, to get out from under, we ought honestly to make sure we don't want it for the wrong reasons.

No one is always safe. No one can know when he may become ill, or have an accident, or find himself in some serious situation. No one knows all the answers. No one can be sure he is self-sufficient.

Besides, others have much invested in us. Others have taught us, trained us, nursed and nourished us, loved us, and given us part of their lives — parents, teachers, doctors, friends, family have done this and much more — and they have a right to an interest in us, and we have an obligation to recognize that right.

There is also the fact that if we are alone and without the interest of others we could become indifferent and deteriorate. Much of our performance is for others and not for us. We do our best when others expect it of us. If life were simply a matter of satisfying our selfish selves, there wouldn't be much progress or improvement· The faith and interest of others leads us to be better — and surely we wouldn't, for the wrong reasons, want to separate ourselves from stabilizing factors and influences, and place ourselves in a position that would make it easier to lower standards or lose the most precious things a person can possess: virtue, honesty, honor, respect, excellence of purpose and performance.

Almost anything can happen to almost anyone, and the "c u t - l o o s e," "get-out-from-under," "leave-me-alone" attitude, in this sense, isn't sensible or safe. To cite a significant sentence: "There is no such thing in human existence as being so high you're not responsible to anybody."[11]

"... not responsible to anybody?"

To repeat this self-evident sentence: "There is no such thing in human existence as being so high you're not responsible to anybody."[11] This applies to all people in all positions. It applies to the attitude (if we should ever be tempted to have it) that we don't need others, that we are self-made, self-sufficient, secure. But no man — no matter what his situation or circumstances — no man knows when he will need another — or when he will need Higher Help.

"There but for the Grace of God am I," is an oft cited sentence. Any of us could find ourselves in urgent need. Any of us could find ourselves in greatly altered circumstances. Furthermore, no one ever reaches the point where he doesn't owe much to many, or where he is accountable only to himself.

The employer and the employed are responsible to each other. Both are responsible to people who buy or use the product. People in the highest or lowest places are in difficulty if others are not working with them. Even in the least free countries and conditions, public opinion, the attitude of people, is important. Even the most absolute in authority cannot stand alone. Whoever he is, he is accountable both to other people and to a Higher Power — as all of us are.

We are indebted to those who work for us and with us; to those who risk their earnings to develop useful products; to those who make employment possible; to those who help make things go successfully, and help to keep society solvent. We are indebted to those who serve us, those who associate with us. We are indebted to those who risk their lives for the enforcement of law.

No matter what sense of sufficiency we may feel, we all have need of others, and we all have reason to give gratitude and recognition, with a sincerely humble sense of responsibility to each other, and to the Father of us all. "There is no such thing in human existence as being so high you're not responsible to anybody." This applies to all people.

The safety of counsel

Young people sometimes decide to go it alone in life. They learn a little and feel they have learned much more, and often fail to ask for counsel because they think they already know the answer — or at least the one they want. But none of us — at any age — is ever so old or so young, so knowledgeable that he knows all the answers.

When a person of much experience and much responsibility fails to seek or accept counsel, he has arrived at a precarious place. And when a person of inexperience feels he doesn't need to listen, doesn't need to learn, he, too, has arrived at a precarious place. "They that will not be counselled," said Benjamin Franklin, "cannot be helped. If you do not hear reason she will rap you on the knuckles."[12]

No one is knowledgeable enough, or has experience enough to think of everything at once, to see all possible meanings in a contract or commitment, or be aware of all the hazards, or see all sides of a subject.

No one should write a letter of serious commitment or put anything into print or make a decision of consequence in matters of marriage or money or career, or be enticed to sign or say yes to any plausible proposition, or make any quick or substantial decision of any kind without considering, reconsidering, and seeking adequate counsel. Successful people need counsel. Unsuccessful people need counsel.

The hasty impulse, the know-it-all attitude, the pride or stubbornness that keep us from asking — these are dangerous approaches to any problem.

From the youngest in years to the oldest of age, there is no one who can be always sure he is right, no one who has learned so much of life that he doesn't need the counsel of others, and a prayerful approach to all problems. There is safety in counsel, no safety without it. "They that will not be counselled, cannot be helped."

On being a good sport

Not infrequently we hear the phrase, "Come on, be a good sport" — or something else that means the same thing. It is sometimes used as an inducement to persuade people to participate in wholesome purposes — for talking people into doing things they should do; and sometimes for unwholesome purposes — for talking people into doing things they shouldn't do. It is the latter misuse of persuasion that is of much concern.

The old saying that misery loves company is often evident as people often try to tempt people to do what others do, to be what others are, even if it means pulling them down to a lower level. Why anyone would try to pull other people down is one of the mysteries of human nature, but in truth it must be said that it is often so.

Often people are pressured to partake of things that would lower their resistance, impair their judgment, damage their minds, and, much worse, their souls, by the persuasive appeal to "Be a good sport." Sometimes girls are dared or induced to partake of or to do that which leads to loss of virtue, by persistent, insidious persuasion. Boys are often dared to lawless, irresponsible, unwise or immoral acts — joining a reckless crowd, risking their records, risking the whole future before them — by the wheedling or even threatening phrase, "Come on, be a good sport" — or something else that means the same.

How it is that doing something dangerous or damaging or degrading is supposed to make a person "a good sport" is never quite clear. Why should anyone think that anyone else should lower his standards, clutter his record, compromise his life to prove he is a so-called good sport? To do so would be sheer stupidity.

Perhaps we should reverse the process. Perhaps we should say this to those who endeavor to induce others to do what they shouldn't do: "Be a good sport, and don't try to dare or tempt other people to do something for which they will surely be sorry. Be a good sport, and don't try to pull other people down to a lower level."

"... you are going to meet again"

"We are all of us fellow-passengers on one and the same planet,"[13] said Hendrick Van Loon. And if we ever behave in a manner that makes it necessary for us to avoid other people, we have made a mistake.

In the first place, the chances of avoiding other people are not very good. So long as we are fellow-passengers on the same planet, there are likely to be meetings face to face. If we have done wrong things or acted in unseemly ways, if we have been dishonest or taken advantage of anyone, or even just plain been unpleasant, the chances are we shall meet our mistakes — again and again, anywhere, anytime.

A successful and colorful character had this to say: "Never act toward someone as though you were never going to come across him again in life. . . . Never sacrifice what the future may hold for some immediate gain. Be yourself with everyone you meet — but be your best self, for you can be sure that before you have lived out your life you are going to meet again."[14]

We don't have to agree with people to get along with them; we don't have to compromise or abandon our own principles, but we do have to be honest, considerate, forthright and fair. The world can become very small and cramped if there is any place we can't go, any street we can't walk on, any crowd we can't mingle with for fear of the embarrassment of seeing someone

[29]

to whom we have been unfair or whom we have offended.

And this is true at any age. We may deal unkindly or unfairly with a child, and in later years find ourselves face to face with the man he has become, and find him in some place or position where we must ask him for some service, or need his help under some circumstances. Besides, it gnaws at us inside if there are people with whom our relationships haven't been altogether honest or with whom we have been unfair, curt, or unkind.

The world becomes very confined, if, because of our misconduct, there are those we feel we have to avoid. In a sense, it is as Edward Fitzgerald said it: "Any road leads to the end of the world."[15] ". . . you are going to meet again."

"You may have to live in a crowd, but you do not have to live like it . . . "

—HENRY VAN DYKE

PART 3

> *"In general those parents have the most reverence who deserve it . . ."*
>
> —SAMUEL JOHNSON

"Life hath quicksands -- life hath snares"

There is a poignant, moving line from Longfellow: "Oh thou child of many prayers! Life hath quicksands — life hath snares!"[16] Young people often wonder why parents worry, why they counsel and caution, why they pray and plead, why parents become concerned. Confidence is an enviable attribute. Self-confidence is a quality to be cultivated. But an innocent or unknowing overconfidence is sometimes difficult and dangerous to deal with.

Remember this: Those who have been over the road are better guides than those who haven't. And parents *have* been over the road — or certainly some of it. They know something of the critical points, of the youthful impulses; of the wise and unwise ties and attachments; of the unguarded times on which life sometimes forever turns. They have seen the road signs.

They know how life sometimes breaks our best laid plans — and sometimes breaks our hearts. They know the need for balance, for temperance, for faith. They also know the tragedies that sometimes come by seeking shortcuts, by running the red lights, by cluttering a record that may keep us from opportunities we might have had. Remember, young friends, imperfect though they may be, parents have a God-given responsibility — plus experience, insight, inspiration, and a love for which there is no absolute substitute from any source. They know that you can lose time, get on a wrong road, quit school, and find yourselves in frustration and regret for the future. They know the pitfalls, the wrong turns, the importance of even some of the simplest, most harmless looking decisions.

Be patient with parents.. Respect them. Confide in them. Love them. Listen to them. Be grateful for those who know enough, who care enough, who love enough, who pray and plead, and counsel and caution, and who would do whatever they honestly could to help you to the highest possibilities of life. Remember there is real reason for the concern of others for us. "Oh thou child of many prayers! Life hath quicksands — life hath snares!"

Take time for your children

In these swift-passing scenes and seasons there seems to come — insistently, almost above all else — this compelling cry: Take time for your children.

More and more, professional people are telling us that children are shaped and molded at a very early age — so early that it is a sobering fact to face. Home, parents, early impressions set the pattern for the future — and the evidence is overwhelming that nothing in this world is ever going to take the place of wholesome, happy homes. And there is more to this than food, shelter, and physical sustenance. There is the shaping of attitudes, of minds, of morals; opening avenues of interest and activity; instilling honesty, respect, reverence; prayers at a mother's knee; correction with fairnes and firmness "showing . . . afterwards an increase of love"[17] and kindness. All this we cannot be, all this we cannot do, by not being there, by living separate lives, by an over-absorption in outside interests. Take time for your children. They are so soon grown, so soon gone.

"Is mother home?" "Where is mother?" are the questions asked when they come home from anywhere. Oh, let them have the blessing of your being there. Take time for open arms; for talking, for reading, for family prayer: for home evenings and hours. As one discerning poet put it: "Richer than I you can never be — I had a mother who read to me."[18] Take time for making memories; for fixing sure foundations that will last long after less essential things are far forgotten.

Mothers need to be home. A mother, a father, waiting is a source of safety and assurance. Parents need to give their children wholesomeness and wholeness by the very lives they live. Oh, the blessedness of coming home and finding mother there, with love and kindness and encouragement.

Life goes quickly. Don't brush them off and turn them over to others. Take time for your children — before they're grown, before they're gone. Oh, take time for your children.

Take time to listen

Besides *seeking* counsel, which all of us need, there is another side of the subject: taking time to listen so that we can *give* counsel sincerely and sensibly.

"Lately I have thought a lot about 'listening,' " said Hannie Struve. "How often you hear a little child complain . . . 'you're not *listening!*' And how easily the mother replies, 'What do you *want?*' And mostly the child does not really 'want' anything, only to communicate."[19]

Take time to listen — to children — young people — others! Sometimes they are reluctant to ask because they receive impatient answers. "Why do we parents so often say, 'I'm busy now' . . ." asked one thoughtful father. "Why do we . . . not realize that a child is like a sunbeam — here for a moment and then gone somewhere else."[20]

Talking — listening — patience, willingness to learn enough before jumping to quick conclusions. Sometimes in just letting them talk and using us for listening, they will come safely to their own conclusions. But when two people both talk at once, when they interrupt each other or when they don't talk at all, there aren't likely to be any helpful answers.

Yes, it takes time to listen, but it takes more time to correct mistakes once they have been made. "Dear Lord, make me a better parent," pleaded Gary Cleveland Myers. "Teach me to understand my children, to listen patiently to what they have to say and to answer all their questions kindly. Keep me from interrupting them, talking back to them, and contradicting them. Make me as courteous to them as I would have them to be to me."[21]

With too many misjudging others, and with too few taking time to listen, counsel cannot seem as satisfactory as it should. "The key is communication," said a thoughtful source. " 'Can't you see I'm busy?' . . . ought to be banned [by parents]. 'Listen' ought to be [implanted] over every parent's heart."[22] If only we could feel we have been heard! If only we would listen when we should!

. . . what men are made of . . .

Phillips Brooks once portrayed what he called "the double parentage of every child born into the world — the heavenly and earthly parentage. Many fathers and mothers who are eager to advance the interest of their children never recognize this dual parentage," he said . "They treat their children as if these children were of their own making . . . oblivious of the fact that the child is also of God's making . . . We owe to our children above all things, . . . room enough to let them develop, . . . according to . . . their temperament, their character, . . . and sometimes their genius."[23]

"A child is not a block of marble, to be hewn out into what you will. A child . . . is a plant which you are to set into the right soil of truth, and then watch as it develops its own special nature."[24]

There is increasing evidence on the importance of loving, teaching, encouraging children from the very earliest years, and all along the whole developing length of life. A child untaught, unencouraged — a child unloved and left too much alone — is likely not to have a very high opinion of himself.

And a child who doesn't have a good opinion of himself is not likely to achieve much. There is an obligation always to help every child, at every age, at every level of life, to have a sincere awareness of his priceless importance and possibilities, to extend his interests and activities, to respect himself and others, and to reach and more fully realize the limitless, everlasting possibilities of life. We must cultivate young minds, all minds, or we shall have dull men. And it is unthinkable that any should be untaught, unloved, unencouraged, or left too much alone. As so well has been said: "A boy is the only known substance from which a man can be made."[25]

"When your heart tells you things your mind does not know"

There is this phrase, cited by a thoughtful friend: ". . . when your heart tells you things your mind does not know."[26] All of us have impressions, promptings, a sense of warning sometimes; an intuition, an awareness, the source of which we do not always know, and we often have to trust our hearts, along with the facts we face.

Life isn't merely a mechanical calculator or a slide rule situation. There is the spirit; the feelings; conscience, convictions; things we know are there; things we know are real; things we can't put in a test tube. Love is one of them. Faith is another; a sense of right and wrong; sometimes a sense of urgency; sometimes a sense of assurance. There is so much that can't be physically touched, so much that can't be mechanically calculated.

Parents often have impressions pertaining to their children. And children often tease parents to let them do things that had better not be done: "Why can't I do this? Why can't I go there? Why? Why?" — questions that parents often cannot answer with full satisfaction, except that they feel it, they know it, with an inner sense of certainty.

As we live for it, wisdom comes from many sources, both within and outside ourselves. And children often have to trust parents, and know that their hearts tell them things their minds do not know. Parents are not perfect, not infallible, but overall, the inspiration, the guidance that comes with prayerful pleading, brings warnings, promptings, impressions from beyond our sight and sound, which no one should stubbornly ignore.

Beyond books, beyond all that we can weigh and measure, beyond all the tangibles that we can touch, there are influences and forces within and outside ourselves that we well would pay attention to. As Shakespeare said it: "There are more things in heaven and earth, Horatio, than are dreamt of in your philosophy."[27] And, so, beloved young people, be patient with parents when they counsel, when they are concerned — when the heart tells them things the mind does not know.

"The most important thing a father can do for his children, is to love their mother."

—AUTHOR UNKNOWN

PART 4

"The supreme happiness of life is the conviction that we are loved."

—Victor Hugo

"Marriage is more than a wedding . . ."

"One of my students wrote me announcing his engagement," said Wm. Lyon Phelps, " 'This is not going to be much of a wedding,' he said, 'but it is going to be a wonderful marriage.' "[28]

This states a simple fact, sometimes overlooked — the fact that marriage is much more than a wedding — infinitely more. And among the foremost facts to be faced is that marriage is made up of the duties and routine and responsibilities of every day — day after day after day — and that marriage is a relationship of two imperfect people — a relationship that requires character, loyalty, common sense, common convictions, along with much giving up of self, and an unfaltering committment to make it a success in the long and enduring sense.

The art of living together happily, is perhaps one of the greatest of all the arts . . ."[29] said Dr. Phelps. "Naturally, . . . all sorts of adjustments are called for."[28] "Quarrels and disputes are sure to come, [but] the great thing is not to let them *last* . . ."[29]

In marriage "two distinct personalities must work toward one end . . . ," said Temple Bailey, "It is not possible for a married couple to reach happiness with eyes fixed on different stars; . . . they must set up a single ideal and work toward

[it] . . . Cease cherishing impossible fancies of impossible futures. Take the best of [your]] dreams and fit them to life as it comes every day."[30] "Divorce is failure."[29]

"The best goal," said an eminent authority, "is the success of the marriage itself."[31] Put all things to that test — and remember that marriage is a relationship of two imperfect people — a relationship that requires character, loyalty, a sense of humor, common conviction, and common sense, along with much giving up of selfishness and self, and unfaltering committment to make it a success in the long and enduring sense.

Marriage is much more than a wedding. "Marriage is a fine and sacred thing if you make it so. . . ."[28]

Has love lasted?"

When asked what was most difficult in marriage — "It's the little things," she said. The little traits and thoughtlessness, the annoying and abrasive trifles all of us seem to have — and if we emphasize the little things, they may become overly large.

When we see a happy marriage — not perfect, but a solid, happy, lasting relationship — we may well ask what the answer is. There is much that makes a marriage. And always, as the years and seasons pass, there comes the question: "Has love lasted? If not," wrote D. Willson, "If not, what has lost it? What has been beautiful? What has been difficult? What has . . . life together given these two, . . . [what has it] taught them?"[32]

Well, it must have taught that little things are often larger than they look: understanding, friendship and companionship along with love — and a little praise and kindness and encouragement.

"Instead of saying to a bride, 'Hold your husband,' . . . we should say, 'Love your husband,'" Margaret W. Jackson said.[33]

And to a man: Be faithful, patient, gentle, kind, considerate — and clean. And there are some other essentials: honesty, truth, common convictions — character. In marriage one c a n scarcely overemphasize character — for without it, likely love won't last. "The most vicious enemy to home life is immorality," said David O. McKay.[34]

"I think we are inclined to forget," said Mrs. Jackson, "that youth and beauty are [after] all . . . only lures. They are not binders . . . We stress too much the externals and forget too much the realities . . . There are greater hazards to marriage than attraction for other people"[33] — quarrelling, pettiness, careless appearance, carelessness in money matters, carelessness in telling the truth. And virtue — always there must be virtue — many virtues — and always there must be forgiving on both sides. With these, with honesty and character, a marriage can survive both the large and little things, and be the most satisfying, the most lasting relationship of life.

Marriage . . . and maturity

"Marriage is for adults only,"[35] wrote one eminent author — not necessarily of years, but maturity of attitude — the maturity to know that there aren't any perfect people, that nothing is ever altogether as anticipated, that the years change us and others. Marriage requires the maturity to adjust, to forgive, to understand, to be forgiven.

Aside from love, attraction, status, whatever else, marriage requires faith, character, companionship, and much in common.

As to faith: "Every venture requires faith."[36] In marriage as in all else, we need "faith in ourselves; faith in others, [but a faith based] upon reasonable grounds."[36]

As to character: marriage requires the character to be moderate, respectful, clean, honest — the character to carry responsibility, to keep commitments, to provide, to honor obligations, to find or make a future.

As to companionship and much in common: marriage requires shared interests, compatible attitudes, and agreement as to standards and basic beliefs.

"Will we always love each other just as we do today?"[36] is a question often asked. "For love to continue it must develop,"[36] to grow it must change. Of course there is change. Who could be so immature as to suppose there would not be change? As you have changed from childhood and through the years of youth, there will be yet further change through the older years of life. "Physical attraction . . . is one element of love . . . but is sure to [change]."[36] And maturity in marriage requires that you love each other not only as you are, but as you will and should and can become. And as to human failings, as to faults: "We all have them . . . and it is only through [love] that we learn to understand."[37]

Marriage requires faith, love, character, companionship, and much in common; the maturity to know that there aren't any perfect people; that there are some who are very wonderful and worthwhile, who can, through all the changes, all the trial and error and even hardship and heartache, bring to marriage the kind of character and understanding that can make of it the most enduring and deeply satisfying relationship of life.

Saving your marriage . . .

Over and over this truth keeps recurring — that marriage and a happy home are the basis of a stable society and a full and happy life. But one of the disillusionments of life is that something once so precious, so promising, could turn, at times, to such incompatibility — and even enmity. "For a couple who have basked in the sunshine of each other's love, to stand by and see the clouds of misunderstanding and discord obscure the lovelight of their lives, is tragedy indeed."[38]

[47]

Part of the answer runs along some lines from Dr. Hubert Howe: "Why don't people know how to stay happily married?" he asked. ". . . What changes so sharply? . . . Men and women, anguished, broken, beseech for some way to rescue the hopes with which they set out . . . hopes so vivid, so sacred, . . . somebody to tell it to, somebody to do it for, somebody that needs you, sombody that shares. . . . What led up to these alleged grounds? Countless petty clashes, ... failures to understand . . . selfishness . . . [failure to be definite and responsible in matters of money] . . . the habit of secrecy . . . lack of common interests [and activities]. . . . Let this drifting apart keep on, and you'll be divorced in spirit if not in court. . . . [Avoid] the growth of drabness . . . Don't let your conversation sink to the dreary level of complaint, anger, self-pity, . . . Don't neglect the tact, politeness . . . compliments . . with which you started out. *Don't let down.* . . . And if you catch yourself brooding on the fact that you've failed to find a perfect mate, just walk up to the mirror and demand, 'Am *I* the perfect mate?' Ask yourself over and over, insistently: 'Am *I* contributing my share, as a partner, to home and happiness?' "[39]

Whatever the cause, whatever it requires, when two people of honor and honesty, of character and common sense, have committed themselves to marriage, saving a home, a family, is worth all the effort.

"Winning a love *once* is not enough. Keep *rewinning* it. . . . In the last analysis, it's up to you to save your marriage."[39]

Quarreling - and happiness at home

One essential element in the joy of living is harmony and happiness at home. And this depends, after all, upon character and courtesy — and just plain common sense. Why, oh why would people who live in this closest of all relationships of life let quarreling and misunderstanding wreck the peace and happiness of home?

"One kind of quarrel clears the air, like a good, sharp thunderstorm, . . ." wrote Dorothy Walworth. "The other kind of quarrel . . . leaves ugly scars and bitterness, which eventually can wreck a marriage. . . . When Ceasar crossed the Rubicon, he could not turn back and have everything the way it was before. . . . If, in quarreling, you call names . . . and show a diabolical ability to use just the words that will hurt most — [if] ruthlessly you rake up all the failings of the past and recklessly destroy even your happiest memories . . . you cannot retrace your steps and have your marriage exactly as it was before. . . . No wife or husband should take too seriously what the other says at the end of an exhausting day . . . [when] weary or tense [or unwell]. . . . Be gentle. In these days, we all have something better to do with our energy than spend it battling with those we love. . . . Don't try to win an argument just for the sake of winning. Your husband or wife is not your rival, not somebody over whom you must have a petty triumph. . . . A quarrel should always be settled. It should not end . . .

with two people sulking for days . . . Somebody should say, 'I'm sorry.' Don't be too proud to say you're sorry. . . . Pride is too expensive. . . . Don't insist on always being in the right. . . . A last word of warning. Keep your quarrels private. Public outbreaks are in the worst possible taste. There is only one remedy for them — shut up!"[40]

It comes down finally to a question of character and courtesy and common sense. Don't be afraid to say you're sorry. And when someone says it sincerely, accept it. Don't let pride or stubborness or stupidity wreck the peace and happiness of a home.

"The real art of conversation is not only to say the right thing at the right place but to leave unsaid the wrong thing at the tempting moment."
—DOROTHY NEVILL

PART 5

"Give us this day our daily work."

—Elbert Hubbard

"I shall not waste my days . . . "

In some moving lines Jack London suggested some attitudes on age, and the fuller use of life: "I would rather be ashes than dust!" he said. "I would rather that my spark should burn out in a brilliant blaze than it should be stifled by dryrot. I would rather be a superb meteor, every atom of me in magnificent glow, than a sleepy and permanent planet. The proper function of man is to live, not to exist. *I shall not waste my days in trying to prolong them. I shall use my time.*"[50]

The cut-off times that men set for themselves, or that others set for them, are not absolute but arbitrary. The work of the world is never done. And it is sad to see someone in idleness or inactivity — waiting — waiting for time to pass. It isn't a question of years or of the clock or calendar, but of each one's working his best, feeling his best; living his best, in satisfying usefulness for the full length of life. And it isn't only a matter of physical effectiveness, but of mind, of spirit, and of judgment and experience in extending ourselves in service.

"The belief that youth is the happiest time of life is founded on a fallacy," said William Lyon Phelps. "The happiest person is the person who

thinks the most interesting thoughts, . . ."[51]
"The wise man," said Seneca, "will always reflect concerning the quality, not the quantity of life."[52]

Life is a stream that moves us silently, certainly, with no stopping place for any of us as we move through time and eternity, with each one to be what he can, and do what he can, through the whole length of life. "The business of life," said Samuel Johnson, "is to go forward."[53]

"I would rather be ashes than dust! I would rather that my spark should burn out in a brilliant blaze than it should be stifled by dryrot. I would rather be a superb meteor, every atom of me in magnificent glow, than a sleepy and permanent planet. The proper function of man is to live, not to exist. I shall not waste my days in trying to prolong them. I shall use my time."

Work - "for thy sake . . ."

One essential for personal peace and a sense of well being is balance — balance of mind, of spirit, of physical effort and refreshment, and not forgetting that work is absolutely essential. But we sometimes forget balance, and are given to going to excesses, from overworking to underworking, from too much too long at work, to too much too long at leisure.

As one example of the back-and-forth swinging

of the cycle, children were once exploited with overwork, and from the deplorable exploiting of child labor, we have seen the excess of over-exploiting leisure — and of young people earnestly wanting work and not finding opportunity enough for wholesome, responsible, productive employment.

It is significant that in the expulsion of Adam and Eve, from Eden, God said: ". . . cursed is the ground for thy sake."[54] Not cursed is man, but cursed is the ground *for thy sake*. Work is a blessing — a physical, mental and spiritual necessity, quite apart from any economic urgency. Everyone needs work — the young, the old: useful occupation, not just busy-work, but sincerely responsible, productive assignments.

And as to the sometimes restlessness and problem of young people, one answer is the opening of opportunities for purposeful employment. Who wouldn't be restless without honest work to do, without feeling needed, without performing a productive part — without useful outlet for mental and spiritual and physical powers in creative accomplishment? One of the greatest services that any individual or organization could perform is to help provide opportunity for useful, worth-while work.

"Work," said Carlyle, "is the grand cure for all the maladies and miseries that ever beset mankind — honest work, which you intend getting done."[55] With so much need in the world, and so much unused and undirected energy, it would seem that one of the most sincere and significant services anyone could offer is to help all who can and will, find useful work in this beloved land.

The poetry of the commonplace

The eminent Sir William Osler expressed a thought that brings routine functions into focus. The "poetry of the commonplace," he called it. "Nothing will sustain you more potently," he said, "than the power to recognize in your humdrum routine, . . . the true poetry of life — the poetry of the commonplace, of the ordinary man, of the plain, toil-worn woman, with their love and their joys, their sorrows and their griefs."[56]

We often glamorize the unusual, the exaggerated, the artificial, but the world goes on, day to day, by the honest, enduring effort of ordinary, faithful people, facing their problems, meeting debts, caring for children, for the sick, caring for each other, performing essential functions, doing their work well, and keeping going against discouragement. And without these wonderful daily doers of what has to be done, this wouldn't be much of a world.

Machines can never altogether take the place of thinking, conscientious, faithfully performing people. Glamor or leisure can never take the place of the solid work of the world, of doing what needs to be done today. "If you do your work with complete faithfulness . . ." said Phillips Brooks, "you are making just as genuine a contribution to the . . . universal good as is the most brilliant worker . . . Oh, go take up your work and do it . . . with cheerfulness and love . . . profoundly devoted to [*your*] work and yet . . . profoundly thankful for the work which other men are doing . . . that everything should reach its best, that every man should do his best in his own line, . . ."[57] To know what has to be done, and then to do it, is not only essential, but often heroic in its own way.

Thank God for sincere and wonderful men, women, children, who do well and honestly what they have to do each day, despite difficulties and disappointments — for faithful people — for simple things — for routine duties — for work well done — for "the poetry of the commonplace."

On growing old usefully

"Use what you have," said Cicero, "and whatever you may . . . be doing, do it with all your might . . . [with your] mind at full stretch like a bow, and never [give] in to . . . age by growing slack. . . . For myself, I had rather be an old man a somewhat shorter time than an old man *before* my time."[58] It is more than twenty centuries since Cicero said it, and his opinion has been supported by many others also.

"Every man's task," said George Emerson, "is his life-preserver."[59] "Let us not try to escape our work . . ." wrote Anna R. Lindsay. "Above all, let us not fail to see it. As long as we live we have work to do. That we are alive today is proof positive that God has something for us to do today. Let us ask ourselves as we arise each morning, What is my work today? We do not know where the influence of today will end. Our lives may outgrow all our present thoughts, and . . . dreams."[60]

"It is important not to lean on other people," said Dolores Del Rio, "because in time you will be unable to do things yourself. . . ."[61] "We should cease fighting age as if it were a foe," said Dr. Sockman "Memories of past experience may be even sweeter than these experiences were in reality . . . when a pleasure is in prospect we are disturbed by the fear it may not be realized. But a pleasure in retrospect is secure."[62] William Cowper left us this: "Absence of occupation is not rest, A mind quite vacant is a mind distressed."[63]

The use of what we have is an obligation. The human mind can do more than it has ever done. The heart is happier when there is something useful to do. The body keeps better health in service. And if we try to save ourselves in inactivity, we lose what we are trying to save. Health and happiness are increased with the physical and mental employment of our powers. As the Country Parson put it: "I don't remember ever seeing a happy man who had nothing to do."[64]

The art of living long . . ."

If we are blessed with long years of life, this brings us to old age, and with old age there sometimes comes concern, not so much concern for growing old gracefully as for growing old usefully — "The Art of Living Long without Growing Old"[65] as one respected person put it.

All reason and sense and inner awareness tell us that men are immortal. But we know what we have here, and we cling to it as long as we can, which always we should and must, seeking to make full use of all the life we live.

As to being well and happy in the later years of life: "A sense of purpose and the opportunity to contribute to others," said one physician, "— these are as vital to total health as are adequate nutrition and rest."[66]

"The happiest person," said William Lyon Phelps, "is the person who thinks the most interesting thoughts . . . As we advance in years we really grow happier, if we live intelligently. . . . To say that youth is happier than maturity is like saying that the view from the bottom of the tower is better than the view from the top. As we ascend, the range of our view widens immensely; the horizon is pushed farther away. Finally as we reach the summit it is as if we had the world at our feet."[51]

Each part of life has its usefulness, its compensations; its challenges, its problems; its beauty, its service, its satisfactions. And as we live in honor, serving, as we can, as fully and in any way we can, keeping faith and peace within ourselves and with Him who made us all, there is an ever added meaning to these lines from Karle Wilson Baker:

> Let me grow lovely, growing old —
>   So many fine things do;
> Laces, and ivory, and gold,
>   And silks need not be new.
>
> And there is healing in old trees,
>   Old streets a glamour hold;
> Why may not I, as well as these,
>   Grow lovely, growing old?[67]

"No man, properly occupied, was ever miserable."

—Letitia E. Landon

PART 6

> "*He who is not ready today will be less so tomorrow.*"

> —Ovid

On seeing children go to school . . .

Seeing children go to school for the first day — or on any other — is reassuring yet sobering. They leave in part the love of home, the influence of family, to enter a new venture from which there is no complete returning at any time. They are taught in many ways by many teachers — taught much that is true, much that proves to be but tentative.

They are exposed to many impressions, many opinions, many personalities — and give up by degrees some elements of child-like innocence, and acquire by degrees some elements of sophistication — moving on to life, never again to be precisely the same — with loving parents knowing they must go, yet wondering — waiting — knowing minds must be disciplined, educated, taught and trained, and conditioned to serve and make their way in the world.

All of this suggests the sobering trust of being a teacher — a teacher of children — a teacher of anyone at all. And always there must be the reminder that there is a wholeness of teachers — and of children. One cannot separate mind and morals; one cannot separate teaching from attitude, from appearance, from personality. What totally makes up the teacher becomes part of the pupil. And so the trust of teaching must include humility, dignity, integrity, respect for truth, the quality of patience, honest fairness, all together adding up to a total of influence and example — remembering that what children see in us or feel from us may be as important as what they hear from us. Being a teacher is more than an occupation or profession. It is a sacred trust.

Seeing children go to school the first day, or any other, is a good yet sobering sight. God bless them every one — and bless and touch the hearts of dedicated teachers who sincerely seek to teach what will benefit and bless for the everlasting length of life — for a teacher is not only an imparter of information; a teacher is a shaper of living souls.

Education -
to what end . . . ?

There is a sentence from Samuel Johnson that points to a persistently important subject: "Integrity *without* knowledge is weak and useless, . . ." he said. "Knowledge *without* integrity is dangerous and dreadful."[68]

We sometimes speak of education as if it were an end in and of itself, but constantly and searchingly we should ask ourselves what *is* the aim of education. Education to what end, for what purpose, is always a compelling question. It is, of course, to increase knowledge and skill, competence and understanding. But it should also increase character and integrity.

To pursue the subject further, suppose we were to educate people for evil and deception. Would an educated evil be more acceptable than an uneducated evil? Certainly it could be more devious and destructive.

We have referred before to talent without character, power without character, weapons without character — even words without character. Anything without character is a hazard, including education without character. Education is surely not a substitute for morality, and in teaching and directing youth, moral and ethical and spiritual elements must be added to give character and balance to their lives, if we are to have a safe and wholesome society.

"The end of education," said President Dickey of Dartmouth, "is to see men made whole, both in competence and in conscience. For to create the power of competence without creating a corresponding direction to guide the use of that power is bad education. Furthermore, competence will finally disintegrate apart from conscience."[69]

We cite a sentence from Henry Adams, who said: "A teacher affects eternity; he can never tell where his influence stops."[70] If moral and ethical content is separated from education, the future would indeed be frightening. "Integrity *without* knowledge is weak and useless. Knowledge *without* integrity is dangerous and dreadful."

On becoming qualified

There is something George Eliot said that has overtones for all of us: "What is opportunity to the man who can't use it?"[71] These words have special meaning for those living in that time of life which is, or should be, a period of preparation. Life goes swiftly. Responsibilities increase. Opportunities to prepare diminish. And one can scarcely conceive of a young person's ignoring the opportunity to develop a talent or skill, to prepare for a tráde, or profession, for a larger role in life.

One could scarcely explain why anyone with opportunity to learn would ever choose to drop out, just to drift, and leave himself open for frustration and disappointment for the future. Life is all we have — life, our hands, our minds, our muscles, our spirit, our willingness to prepare, our willingness to work. Oh, if only we could implant in the minds and hearts of young people the blessing of an education, the blessing of choosing some good goal and moving toward it, the blessing of becoming qualified, and avoiding the disappointments that come later in life when demand for the untrained shrinks, as the economic cycle shifts.

Life, mind, time, talents — these are tools, these are instruments that should be sharpened as soon as possible for enduring and increasing and satisfying service. "The secret of success . . ." said Disraeli, "is for a man to be ready for his opportunity when it comes."[72]

If there are any whom we could reach and touch at this time, we would plead with every young person to pursue his education, his preparation, and improve himself to the finest point possible; to acquire competence, to qualify for life, for learning, for living; to know something well, to do something well, to have something to offer;

to avoid being a marginal person, to be more useful to family, community, country, and also serve himself, and have the great satisfaction that comes with being needed, wanted, appreciated, compensated. "What is opportunity to the man who can't use it?"

"Everything counts in the long run . . . "

There is a phrase from somewhere that says: "Everything counts in the long run." This applies to all that goes into the making of a life, the influences, decisions, examples, from earliest years. "Everything counts in the long run," and the record matters very much.

People build their confidence in us — or lack of it — by how our words square with the facts. If what we say proves to be true, it increases the confidence of others in us. If what we say proves false, or partly so, it diminishes the confidence of others in us. If we pretend to be something we aren't or take credit for what we haven't done, ultimately this becomes known. There is no way of erasing the trail of life, no way of going back and obliterating the impressions and misimpressions we may have left in many places.

People may believe in our repentance; they may forgive us; they may be lenient and charitable — but our lives are the composite of what we have thought and done and said — all of which ought to square with the facts, whatever they are. "Everything counts in the long run."

Our record of meeting obligations, our record in school, at work, at home, with friends and family; our record of honor and honesty, of cleanliness and truthfulness all add up to the total of what we are. And whatever we are, others will ultimately know. Every position we acquire, every opportunity that opens, sooner or later depends upon some person's impression or appraisal of us — and upon what we are.

Sooner or later the true and the false face each other in a record that is written in the minds and opinions and impressions of other people — and within ourselves. Sooner or later the truth or untruth becomes apparent. "If it is not right," said Marcus Aurelius, "do not do it; if it is not true, do not say it."[73] "Everything counts in the long run."

Careers -- Credentials -- Competence

T There are pressing and important decisions that many must make — concerning school, careers, credentials, competence — a subject always timely for those who are tired, and who, while tired, may make some shortsighted decisions. It may also be time to say something to those who have dropped out along the way, before they were as fully qualified as they could be or should be — those who have decided they're all through so far as further training is concerned — and who may have decided this too soon.

Increasingly it is apparent that muscles are really not enough, and that an untrained mind, however good, is not enough. It is a time when the demand diminishes for those less skillful, less competent, less technically trained. But it is also a time when the opportunities and openings are limitless for the minds and hands of those who are willing to learn and to discipline themselves.

With knowledge, skill, character, mental and manual facility, there are limitless ways for a person to make a happier usefulness for himself, a better life for loved ones, and to give a greater service to community and country.

It is good to be willing to work, but better to be prepared to work at something specific. And all who too soon have supposed they have learned enough, done enough, so far as competence is concerned, would well ask themselves what they would *really* like to be, what they would *really* like to be doing, five years from now, or ten, or maybe more.

As long as we live, we'll be doing something with life. It may be something we like or something we dislike. It may be something that is needed, or something not very much needed. And the rewards generally will be measured according to competence, and so will the satisfactions.

Time goes no matter what we do with it, whether we use it to prepare and skillfully perform, or use

it to putter and loaf along. Those who are looking ahead at life had just as well decide to be
something they want to be, to make the effort,
to stay with it, to qualify for it, and not rely on
hazy hopes. Decide to "Make the most of yourself, for that is all there is to you."[1]

"*Where one succeeds because
of his smartness, ten succeed because of their faithfulness.*"

—AUTHOR UNKNOWN

PART 7

> *"Think what you do when you run in debt; you give to another power over your liberty. . . . It is hard for an empty bag to stand upright."*
>
> —BENJAMIN FRANKLIN

If we are running
deeply into debt . . .

There is a somewhat mundane matter which calls for comment because it concerns conscience and character, and certainly self-respect. We are referring to the down-drag of an over-due debt, and the self-respect of solvency. This in turn concerns some basic relationships of life.

Many marriages run into trouble because of matters of money. Many people run out on responsibilities because of matters of money. Many people avoid other people because of matters of money. Many are worried, unhappy, deeply concerned because of matters of money. And if we are running deeply into debt, unless we change direction we shall run more deeply into debt.

Good management in money matters is always important, not forgetting thrift, working, saving; and remembering, before we commit ourselves to pay something, that we shall, by all the means we can, do our best to see it through, and not incur a needless debt without some reasonable assurance of being able to meet it when it comes due.

There is this searching question from the Master of mankind: "For which of you, intending to build a tower, sitteth not down first, and counteth the cost, whether he have sufficient to finish it? Lest haply, after he hath laid the foundation, and is not able to finish it, all that behold it, begin to mock him, saying, this man began to build, and was not able to finish."[74]

The money we owe represents someone else's work, someone else's effort, someone's saving, someone's giving up something he might have had. Whenever we don't pay a debt we take something, somehow, from someone — and so should always consider the ability to repay before borrowing. Sometimes situations appear impossible, and the law gives relief; but we shouldn't use it lightly to escape our commitments.

We ought to keep our word, to keep our credit, to keep our trust, to keep the confidence of others in us, to the best of our ability. "For which of you, intending to build a tower, sitteth not down first, and counteth the cost, whether he have sufficient to finish it?"

"The insatiable demand for more"

There is a phrase that suggests a subject: "The insatiable demand for more."[75] Who ever heard of anyone who was happy, who couldn't be satisfied? — who always had to have more and ever more — more thrills, more indulgence, more power, more possessions.

Some over-indulge by trying to satisfy appetites that remain unsatisfied. Some make demands, and when their demands are met, make more demands.

There are communities that want more and more — more size, more reaching for comparative place, and in the process, complicate their problems.

The comparative and competitive spirit often enters in, and insists that the curve, the graph, the record must be ever and always up — which, if for a good purpose, is good — but which, if never satisfied, even after the purpose is satisfied, may be merely the insatiable demand for more. Even when there are more comforts and conveniences than kings could once have had, often there are still demands for more.

Perhaps it comes down finally to a balance of contentment and purpose and peace, with a little wholesome discontent to keep us learning, moving, reaching, producing, but not just more and more without limit, without peace or real purpose. "All the good things of the world are no further good to us than as they are of use," said Daniel DeFoe, "and of all we may heap up we enjoy only as much as we can use, and no more."[76]

That human wants are, in a sense, insatiable, is part of what makes progress possible; but if we drink without quenching thirst, if we rush and run without knowing why we rush and run, we may merely be pursuing the insatiable demand for more.

In all our rushing, striving, struggling, God grant us gratitude, balance, judgment; a solid sense of values, an inner peace, and an honest appraisal of our purpose.

Opposite influences

Two influences often pull in opposite directions upon every person: the pursuit of pleasure and the performance of duty. And in these is the happiness or unhappiness of a whole lifetime, even an everlasting life.

If a person follows his whims, his undisciplined appetites, pleasures, passions, his life will be less, and in some measure lost. If he honors commitments, commandments, and disciplines himself to find pleasure in doing what he knows he ought to do, then he can have many things in one: pleasure, accomplishment, self-respect and the peace of an approved and quiet conscience.

In the routine of work, in professional service, in marriage, in the home, in rearing and caring for a family, there are all degrees of discipline and of facing up to facts, and sometimes, tragically, of trying to run away from facts. But peace and strength, character and accomplishment, happiness and self-respect, come with doing duty, with facing up to facts.

If we make a contract, a covenant, a commitment, sincere and lasting satisfactions follow in seeing things through. It is so with debt, commitments in marriage, caring for children, loyalty to loved ones, to all the obligations of life.

"On the one side," said Samuel Smiles, "are conscience, [duty] and the knowledge of good and evil; on the other indolence, selfishness, love of pleasure, or passion. The weak and ill-disciplined may remain suspended for a time between these influences; but at length the balance inclines one way or the other, . . . A man can only achieve strength of purpose by the action of his own free-will. . . . He can avoid falsehood, and be truthful; he can shun sensualism, and be continent; he can turn aside from doing a cruel thing, and be benevolent, [or the opposite] . . . All these . . . come within the range of self-discipline. And it depends upon men themselves whether in these respects they will be free, pure, and good, on the one hand; enslaved, impure, and miserable on the other."[77]

The world owes me a living . . . ?

There is this — so often said — or supposed: "The world owes me a living." But when God gave man the earth He said, ". . . subdue it."[78] And subduing a world takes work. It was not intended that we should have all the earth has to offer, without effort. Work is a blessing, an absolute essential.

But who or what is this world that is supposed to owe all of us everything? Surely parents owe children love and care and encouragement — providing for and teaching and training. Surely children owe parents respect and love and kindly attention, and care, as may be needed — especially later in life. No parent should be left in loneliness. And surely men owe other men compassionate service and assistance. But if we are speaking of this wonderful planet, it is very impersonal. And it will not produce everything for all of us — or for any of us — without work.

But if when we say the world owes us a living, we are talking about people, this is all of us together. And all of us owe it to ourselves to make the most of ourselves. And since there are always those who, in one way or another, are unable fully to care for themselves, we need to produce more than we consume, and everyone who can should do all he can. But it isn't reasonabel for anyone simply to sit down and say, "The world owes me a living."

There is no magic about it. Someone has to think; someone has to plan; someone has to save; someone has to plow and plant; someone has to manage. Someone has to do everything. Everything has to be done. Nothing does itself.

Someone has to produce or pay for everything in one way or another. There is an exchange of values in all relationships of life, and instead of saying the world owes me a living, this could be a very good time to say thank God for being alive, for opportunity, and for the willingness to make the most of it.

> . . . For great and low there's but one test
> 'Tis that each one shall do his best,
> Who works with all the strength he can,
> Shall never die in debt to man.[25]

. . . if everyone must watch everyone . . .

There is a simple, old fashioned subject that is urgently essential, and that is this: simple honesty There is no credit, no contract, no transaction, no situation that is safe without the element of honesty.

If no one does what he says he will do, no one could count on anything. If everyone has to worry about every property, every possession — watch it, guard it, almost sit on it in a sense, in trying to hold what he has — the world wouldn't run, and life would approach the impossible.

Nobody can watch *everybody* all the time. Nobody can watch *anybody* all the time. No one can stay awake all the time. No one has the time, the strength, the ability to protect himself against all forms of deception and deceit.

No one can know enough in all things always to make safe decisions. We have to trust the physician for his prescription, the pharmacist who fills it, the person who makes things, who sells things and certifies that they are of a certain kind and quality. Few of us, for example, could buy a diamond and know what it was worth. We have to trust someone.

If we can't find a package where we put it; if goods disappear from the shelves; if a car on the street isn't safe; if expense accounts are padded; if we can't leave a piece of equipment with someone to repair, and know he will do only what is needed, and charge only what is fair; if people increasingly deal in deception, there will be less and less peace and progress.

Beyond the boldness of robbery, of burglary and embezzlement, any deception is dishonest: overcharging, getting paid for what we haven't done, taking what isn't ours, saying what isn't so, pretending what we aren't, reporting what we haven't done. In short, if everyone must watch everyone, if no one can trust anyone, there is no safety, no assurance.

If it isn't true, don't say it. If it isn't right, don't do it. If it isn't yours, don't take it. If it belongs to someone else, return it. Honesty is not only the best policy, but a principle, and an absolute essential for the good and happy living of life.

"When we go too far it is seldom in the right direction."

—ANONYMOUS

PART 8

> *"Endure, and keep yourselves*
> *for days of happiness."*

—VERGIL

For the down and discouraging days . . .

Among the realities of life is this: that all people have problems, that all have disappointments, that all have need to be understood, to be encouraged, and at times to be looked upon with compassion. We all wrestle with reality, with conscience, with disappointment, with discouragement — with days on which our spirits are down. This none escape. Yet always there is reason to hold on, to try again, to have faith, to live through the down and discouraging days.

"It is strange indeed to analyze the alternations of depression and exhilaration which haunt us like a summer cloud," wrote Gamaliel Bradford, ". . . day *before* yesterday, it seemed to me there was no life left in me; exertion, existence was a burden; work, to which I always turn, knowing that patient perseverance with it will distract if not console, lost its charm. . . . But the curious thing is that *yesterday* was no better, in fact, worse, if anything; but my condition was wholly different. I have plenty of these down moods. I suppose everyone has. . . . The lesson I strive to learn, the lesson which appears so easy, but is so hard, is to remember in the down times that they will not last and that the up times will return."[79]

Darkness never had the last word. Always again there is another day. Always, eternally, there is hope and faith — and tomorrow morning. And this assurance should give us reason to hold on, to wait, to try again, to believe, to hold to hope.

In the words of John Milton, "Bear up, and steer right onward,"[80] — even on the down days. And to all of us it suggests the patient understanding of the moods and problems of other people. As Alexander Pope so sincerely said it:

> Teach me to feel another's woe,
> To hide the fault I see;
> That mercy I to others show,
> That mercy shown to me.[81]

... *Tomorrow morning* ...

"Though we sometimes speak of a primrose path," said John Erskine, "we all know that a bad life is just as difficult, just as full of obstacles and hardships, as a good one. . . . The only choice is in the kind of life one would care to spend one's efforts on."[82] This is reminiscent somewhat of what our Savior said, that the rain falls on "the just and on the unjust."[83]

"Alas!" said George Macdonald, "how easily things go wrong. . . ."[84] *And they do.* Life is difficult at times for all of us. But it is difficult in different ways, depending upon attitude, upon standards; depending upon what our objectives are. A person can have sorrow from doing what he knows he shouldn't do — almost, in a sense, a self-inflicted sorrow, that can be bitter and debasing. Or he can have a sorrow or setback that comes while doing something it seemed he should do; yet, with all the depth of disappointment, the bitterness and self-blame can be absent.

A line from Lord Avebury touches the edge of the subject: — "If we are ever in doubt what to do," he said, "it is a good rule to ask ourselves what we shall wish on the morrow that we had done."[85]

J. Reuben Clark Jr., used to speak of "the thrill of a moment, and a lifetime of regret." There is much bitterness and blame in deliberately doing something bad — in the headlong, downhill misdoing that goes nowhere to nothing that anyone in his right mind would ever really want. And well would we pause to ask ourselves honestly — always — what would we wish we had done — or hadn't done — tomorrow morning?

To go back to John Erskine: "Though we sometimes speak of a primrose path, . . . a bad life is just as difficult, just as full of obstacles and hardships, as a good one." Not just as, we might add, but more so —in its bitter self-blaming regret. Since this is so, why not decide to live a good life, with peace and gratitude, and without the bitterness and embarrassment of tomorrow morning?

Discouragement comes
to all of us . . .

Discouragement is said to be one of the most effective tools of the devil. And "Despondency," said De Witt Talmage, "is the most unprofitable feeling a man can indulge in."[86]

All of us begin many good things, which, because of discouragement, we fail to finish — and so we lose time in false starts and premature stops. And if anyone wanted to see us waste our lives, he wouldn't have to tempt us to do something too obviously sinful. He would only have to discourage us to the point of giving up doing what we should be doing, and make us feel that we were failures. Thus much of life would be wasted.

And yet discouragement comes to all of us. No one ever conquered a bad habit without discouragement and without earnest effort. No one ever acquired an adequate education or any real competence without discouragement and purposeful practice and persistence. No one has ever lived without discouragement. We grow by doing, by enduring, and not giving in to the first difficulty.

"Whatever the situation, . . ." said Dr. Fosdick, "and however . . . disheartening it may be, it is a great hour when a man ceases adopting [difficulties] as an excuse for despondency and tackles himself as the real problem. No mood need be his master. . . . Remember others. Emotions are contagious . . . [and] can infect a whole household."[87]

As each day brings its "petty round of irritating concerns and duties, help us to play the man," pleaded Robert Louis Stevenson, "help . . . us to go on our business all this day, bring us to our resting beds weary and content and undishonored, and grant us in the end the gift of sleep."[88] And finally, as Ian Maclaren said it: "Let us be kind to one another, for most of us are fighting a hard battle. . . ."[89]

"... opposition in all things"

A question asked by H. G. Wells suggests a subject: "What on earth would a man do with himself," he said, "if something did not stand in his way?"[90] Sometimes when life is difficult and discouraging, when we feel that people or circumstances are against us, when we are running against resistance, we might well ask ourselves what we would do if there weren't some resistance to run against. "Man, without opposition or competition, would loaf out his life and die a limpid lump of flesh,"[25] said one observer.

This suggests some aspects of the experience of people in space, where things are relatively loose and free and frictionless, and where the need for exercise and exertion is emphasized. A muscle won't develop if there is nothing to work against. Without work, even hearts would cease to function effectively. We couldn't even start or stop if it weren't for friction. We couldn't get traction, and brakes wouldn't work.

These physical facts have their counterpart in matters of morale, in matters of mind, in matters of the inner resources of man — the ability to endure, to develop. Often we would wish that learning weren't so long and difficult and demanding. But if we don't have something to push against we never develop any push.

The mind wouldn't develop if there were no problems to wrestle with, nothing to solve, nothing to think through. Character wouldn't develop if there were no decisions or choices to make or obstacles to overcome. "For it must needs be, that there is an opposition in all things"[91] — opposition and effort, in learning and doing and enduring. And even though some days are discouraging and some situations seem too difficult, it is the overcoming that makes men.

To cite a sentence from a screenplay: "If we don't try we don't do, and if we don't do, what are we on this earth for?"[92] To repeat the question of H. G. Wells: "What on earth would a man do with himself if something did not stand in his way?"

. . . to see something get going . . .

"Life," said Benjamin Disraeli, "is a tumble-about thing of ups and downs,"[93] — "with its sick hurry, its divided aims . . ."[94] Matthew Arnold added. There are times when all of us feel overburdened, with debts, with obligations, so many things undone, so many undone things to do — worries, problems, and sometimes our share, it seems, of sorrows. And we wonder how we can be everywhere we ought to be, do all we ought to do, meet the obligations, and carry the weight of our worries, as we seem to divide ourselves in too many different directions, too many ways at once — not feeling that we are completing or disposing of or quite in control of anything — just a re-shuffling of papers, a re-shuffling of problems.

To all of this, some gentle advice from an unnamed source proposes the "one-at-a-time" approach: "Mountains viewed from a distance," it says, "seem to be unscalable, but they *can* be climbed, and the way to begin is to take the first upward step. From that moment the mountains are less high. The slopes that seem so steep from a distance seem to level off as we near them."[25]

Any task in life is easier if we approach it with the one-at-a-time attitude. One step — a beginning — doing something about something, beginning to see something get going — gives assurance that we are on our way and that the solving of problems is possible. To cite a whimsical saying: "If you chase two rabbits, both of them will escape."[25] No one is adequate to everything all at once. We have to select what is important, what is possible, and begin where we are, with what we have. And if we begin — and if we keep going — the weight, the worry, the doubt, the depression will begin to lift, will begin to lighten.

We can't do everything always, but we can do something *now*, and doing something will help to lift the weight and lesson the worry. "The beginning," said Plato, "is the most important part."[95]

"*I see not a step before me as I tread on another year;*
But I've left the Past in God's keeping, — the Future His mercy shall clear;
And what looks dark in the distance may brighten as I draw near."

—Mary Gardiner Brainard

PART 9

"There is another man within me that's angry with me."

—Thomas Browne

How to cure
a bad conscience . . .

"The voice of conscience," said Madame de Stael, "is so delicate that it is easy to stifle it; but it is also so clear that it is impossible to mistake it."[96] "Conscience," said Francis Bowen, "is a divine voice in the human soul . . ."[97]

In a sense it is a voice within, and yet also something from outside. George Crabbe referred to conscience as "man's most faithful friend!"[98] — a friend that "warns us as a *friend* before it punishes as a judge."[99]

Some have thought they could conquer conscience by ignoring it, by wearing it down, by acting as if it weren't there But the persistent offender loses the finer sensitivities of life; the sense of acceptance to himself, to God, and to others also — and the peace he might have had. Those who choose to live as if they had no conscience in some way or other pay a price. Conscience is like a nerve system. If we deaden it, it doesn't tell us the truth, and if we don't know the truth we are in trouble.

There are some things a person simply cannot partake of and still remain as he was. Every deliberate and determined act against conscience somehow changes a person inside. The law of compensation still moves in matters of conscience, as in all else, and despite all talk about changing principles, commandments, morality and immorality, man cannot act contrary to the inner responses God has given, cannot ignore the whisperings from the Divine Source, without the consequences that follow when we deny the better things we know.

We cannot ignore conscience without coarsening ourselves, and well would we listen to it as a friend before it becomes a tormentor. The only way to cure a bad conscience is to stop doing what we know we shouldn't do, and start doing what we should do.

"There are two who will know . . . "

"When I left my home to go away to school," said a thoughtful son, "my father said to me: 'No matter what you think or what you do, there are *two* who will know — you and the Father of us all.'"

This may not have a very modern sound, but it answers some questions. Even if all the world doesn't know, even if our family and friends don't know, there are still *two* who know. And even if there were only *one* — even for those who don't acknowledge an eternal record, a living God and personal relationship to Him — still

— *I* know — *you* know — each man knows that which concerns himself.

Now, as to the questions, or one of them at least: With people breaking the commandments, or not acknowledging them: departing from honesty, virtue, morality; setting aside time-honored standards and restraints; doing just what they want to do, supposedly — or at least doing as they profess to please — well, if they are living just like they want to live, why aren't they happy? Why are they still arguing with themselves inside — and with others — uneasy, feeling cheated, unsatisfied, with a gnawing accusation inside themselves? Elbert Hubbard gave one answer when he said, "Men are punished by their sins, not for them."[100]

In a sense, such laws enforce themselves. By his very nature man is what he is. And if he lives one way he gets one result. If he lives another way he gets another result. It is true that people have been variously taught and conditioned by teaching and training, but there is something basic that works within, as we run with or against the light — and men become refined or coarse, easy or uneasy, happy or unhappy, self-respecting or self-accusing by how they live their lives.

There is only one way to find personal peace and an inner respect, and it can't be done by living against the counsel God has given. To return to the opening sentence: "No matter what you think or what you do, there are *two* who will know" — and even if there were only *one*, it still wouldn't be a very good gamble.

"How could I face my children . . . ?"

This was heard from a wonderful, forthright grandfather. He had just talked with a young grandson — one of those searching sessions when a child asks direct, innocent questions — when a child with steady eyes and innocent honesty could make a man earnestly examine himself to see if he detects any deception within his own soul. And then this honest, grateful grandfather asked a simple question: "How could I face my children, my grandchildren and tell them I had done wrong?" Don't try to hide your heart from a boy. "Boys," wrote Emerson, "know truth from counterfeit as quick as a chemist does."[101]

Too often we hear of abuse of children: cruelty, corruption. One can scarcely conceive of this being so, and it reminds us of this sobering indictment from our Savior: ". . . whoso shall offend one of these little ones . . . it were better for him that a millstone were hanged about his neck, and that he were drowned in the depth of the sea."[102] It is something to think of.

Children come here clean and sweet and teachable, from the Father of us all. Innocent they come, and innocent they are, until environment or example is otherwise. "The mind," said William Ellery Channing, "like the body, depends upon the climate it lives in, on the air it breathes."[103] Heaven help those who abuse or neglect or corrupt, or are cruel to children, or who are indifferent to the environment that takes their innocence from them. Children have a right to be protected from exploitation and from evil influence. "I have commanded you to bring up your children in light and truth."[104]

"How could I face my children — anyone's children — and tell them I had done wrong?" Lord, help us to live to feel clean and comfortable with honest, innocent children, and with others also, and with our own souls inside.

When I do good . . .

We still remember the voice saying most sincerely: "A sweet feeling comes into my heart when I do the things I know are right." Since the universe is run by law, since nature lives by law, since all the physical environment of man, all he makes, and all results are realized by law, there is no reason to suppose that the well-being of the mind and spirit of man is not also subject to the laws of life. There is an inner sense, an inner action, a result realized by the laws of right and wrong.

A clean man has a sense of peace and self-respect; an unclean man does not. A fair man has a sense of assurance and acceptance; an unfair man does not. A kind man has a sense of well-being with himself and others; an unkind man punishes himself as he punishes others. A truthful man doesn't have so much difficulty in remembering what he said; an untruthful man may have much difficulty in trying to remember what he said. Call it conscience, call it right or wrong, call it a God-given inner sense, or whatever you will, but there are responses, results, by laws kept, by laws broken, in the physical, mental, spiritual makeup of men.

True, men's thinking is conditioned by what they have been taught, by harsh or gentle circumstances, by those they deal with, by the honor or dishonor of others, by what may sometimes be considered necessity — and yet, in the overall, irrevocable law is endlessly operative. And simple though it seems, and naive, some would suppose, to say so, yet sincerely as we seek to be and do better, there is peace of mind, refinement of soul. Yet if we seek to take advantage of others, to live against the commandments, the virtues, the time honored morals, we fight and quarrel with ourselves inside, and coarsen ourselves and become less kind — all of which seems summarized in this sentence from Abraham Lincoln: "When I do good I feel good. When I don't do good I don't feel good."[4]

Despite all variations, arguments and explanations, always and forever, it is sincerely that simple: "When I do good I feel good. When I don't do good I don't feel good."

A lesson from Huckleberry Finn

Concerning this matter of a supposed emancipation from morality, may we forthrightly face and reaffirm this fundamental fact: that unhappiness, frustration, and impairment of the minds and lives of young and old alike, come with failure to keep the commandments.

Explain it any way you will, in technical or in commonplace terms, or in the jargon of those who want to rid themselves of all restraint, yet it all adds up to an overwhelming evidence that in this we are dealing with eternal truths, and that men cannot escape the consequences of their own conduct — that, indeed, they pay a heavy price when they degrade their bodies, minds, and morals.

Well, we cannot leave it there. There has to be an answer — and there is: The answer is the simple, honest process of repentance. But to be relieved of any burden at all, a person's repentance must go deep beyond the surface — a repentance that is honestly sincere — an actual change of heart, of life; a real and literal departure from the errors of the past. And those who try to lift the load in any other way will *not* find the peace they so much seek.

This point is made by Mark Twain as, in ungrammatical language, this simple, honest message comes from Huckleberry Finn: "It made me shiver," he said. "And I about made up my mind to pray and see if I couldn't try to quit being the kind of boy I was and be better. So I kneeled down. But the words wouldn't come. Why wouldn't they? It warn't no use to try and hide it from Him. . . . I knowed very well why they wouldn't come. It was because my heart warn't right, it was because I warn't square, it was because I way playing double. . . . I was trying to make my mouth *say* I would do the right thing and the clean thing, . . . but deep down in me I knowed it was a lie, and He knowed it. You can't pray a lie — I found that out."[105]

So much for a lesson learned by Huckleberry Finn —a lesson all of us must sometime learn.

"If I were sure God would pardon me, and men would not know my sin, yet I should be ashamed to sin, because of its essential baseness."

—PLATO

PART 10

> "*A man reveals his character even in the simplest thing he does.*"

> —Jean de la Bruyere

. . . without character

Talent without character is always a cause of concern. Anything without character is a cause of concern: money without character, authority without character, power, personality, eloquence, beauty without character, marriage without character, knowledge, teaching without character, weapons, even bare hands without character, even life — or anything without character is a cause of concern.

"Men may know what is right," said Samuel Smiles, "and yet fail . . . to do it; they may understand duty but not summon the resolution to perform it. . . . Many are the valiant purposes . . . that end merely in words; deeds intended, that are never done;" and all for want of character. "There are those who are ready to be unprincipled and unjust rather than unpopular . . . It is much easier to stoop, to bow, and to flatter [with] servile pandering to popularity than to be manly . . . Consciences have become more elastic. . . . So many persons of promise disappoint the expectations of their friends. They march up to the scene of action, but at every step their courage oozes out. . . . Personal beauty soon passes; but beauty of mind and character increases . . ."[106]

There are those who "spend their time in debating just how wrong things are, which, whether they be more or less wrong, . . . [they] know

that it is not for them to do."[107] It is wasteful
to sit by until we have decided "just whether
the thing is wrong, and just how wrong it is."[107]
We need standards, courage, commitments —
and character to keep them.

"Who are the men who have succeeded in the
best way?" asked Phillips Brooks. "They are
men who . . . [knew that] they had their own
duties, . . . their own work to do, and [found a]
way to do it; . . ."[107]

Talent without character, beauty, money, power,
influence, eloquence — anything without character — is a hazard and a cause of concern.
Character will always be found the best safe-
guard of virtue — and of all else that makes life
safe and satisfying.

"Infinite kindness . . . "

Red Barber reminds us of one overall quality
that Branch Rickey said a man must have
if he were to marry one of the famous baseball
manager's daughters. Well, one could imagine
a long list of all the virtues and attributes that
would be required: honor, ambition, talent,
money, social acceptance, and all the others.
But the one quality absolutely required was
this: Infinite kindness.[108]

Kindness might seem to be secondary, but it
quickly broadens out on a wide base. If a person is sincerely kind he wouldn't deceive, he
wouldn't hurt, he wouldn't make unhappy. If
a person is sincerely kind he wouldn't disappoint

a loved one by being dishonest, disloyal, unfaith-
ful. Immorality is not kind — not to others or
ourselves. Dishonesty is not kind — not to anyone. Lack of support, lack of encouragement,
lack of cooperation, are not kind. Infinite kindness includes consideration, compassion, loyalty
— and increases love.

Oh, how many hearts have been broken, how
many lives have been blighted by the cruelty of
unkindness! Yet how many marriages have been
saved, how many sorrows softened by the quality
of kindness! Kindness would respect, care for,
comfort. Kindness would bring people closer.
Kindness would hallow a home, even in the
presence of many problems.

The Master of mankind spoke sharply at times,
and rebuked as occasion required, but it is not
recorded that he was unkind ever to a sincere
or repentant person.

One wouldn't want a son, a daughter, a child
committed in any way to anyone who was cruel
or unkind. Kindness would surely have to be
high among the qualities of a husband, a wife, a
child, a parent — or any acceptable person.
Infinite kindness — it could save a marriage.
It could bring out the best; it could cover for
many other qualities.

Oh the kind words we give shall in memory live
And sunshine forever impart.
Let us oft speak kind words to each other;
Kind words are sweet tones of the heart.[109]

A word called
compassion . . .

There is a word in our language that is called
compassion — a sense of sympathy, a sense of
fellowship in feeling, a sense of others' suffering
— and it puts us in mind of some lines from
Longfellow: "The little I have seen of the world
teaches me to look upon the errors of others in
sorrow, not in anger," he said. "When I take the
history of one poor heart that has sinned and
suffered, and think of the struggles and temptations . . . the brief . . . joy, the feverish inquietude
of hope and fear, the pressure of want, the de-
sertion of friends, I would fain leave the erring
soul of my fellow-man with Him from whose
hands it came."[110]

Oh, how little we are able to judge, and how
much of a mixture are all men: strength intermixed with weakness, courage with fear, good
with bad; all of us with problems, sorrows; with
feelings, hopes, disappointments; all of us mis-
judged, misunderstood at times, all of us misjudging, misunderstanding others — sometimes
generous; sometimes doing, sometimes shrinking
from duty; sometimes at peace, sometimes quarreling with conscience; sometimes patient, sometimes giving way to temper; all of us at times
with human ills, misfortunes, loss of loved ones;
all sometimes discontented, and sometimes feeling blessed and grateful, and all of us resolving
more than we do.

And in thoughtful moments there comes to mind

that we *are* fellow passengers on the same planet — a beautiful and provident planet from Him who gave us life and eternal purposes to pursue. And so at this more mellow moment, the plea for understanding, for patience, for compassion — to trample no one, to injure no one, to deceive no one; to live so that others are safe in our hands; to lift other men's lives in their sickness, in their sorrow, in their loss and loneliness — to lift those who are discouraged and disillusioned with life.

"The little I have seen of the world teaches me to look upon the errors of others in sorrow, not in anger. When I take the history of one poor heart that has sinned and suffered, . . . I would fain leave the erring soul of my fellow-man with Him from whose hands it came."

Cooling tempers . . .

"When a man is wrong and won't admit it, he always gets angry."[111] "The height of human wisdom," said Daniel Defoe, "is to bring our tempers down to our circumstances — and to make a calm within, under the weight of the greatest storm without."[76] Controlling tempers and maintaining calm inside, against turbulent outside events, isn't always easy.

So much is done these days in anger — and it is interesting to note that concerning the first mortal man in serious trouble it was said: "Cain was very wroth."[112] "Anger is the most danger-ous of all passions;" said Seneca, — "the most unmannerly; — Reason deliberates before it judges; — but anger passes sentence without de-liberation . . . it leaves no place for counsel, or friendship, honesty, or good manners; . . . it falls many times upon the wrong person; upon the innocent, [and] tears all to pieces. It is most certain that we might govern our anger, if we would;" he continued, "for the same thing that [angers] us at home, gives us no offense at all abroad; and what is the reason? We are patient in one place, and [not] in another.[113]

"Men should not suffer reverses and unpleasant circumstances to sour their natures," said Brig-ham Young, "and render them fretful and un-social at home, speaking words full of bitterness . . . to their wives and children, creating gloom and sorrow in their habitations, making them-selves feared rather than beloved by their fam-ilies."[114]

"The end of anger is sorrow."[113] "Keep cool and you command everybody."[115]

These brief and moving lines from George Her-bert most earnestly suggest themselves in sum-mary, to husbands, wives; parents, children; friends, neighbors, and associates in all relation-ships of life:

> Throw away thy rod,
> Throw away thy wrath; . . .
> Take the gentle path.[116]

The boomerang:
it does come back . . .

On the question of justice and injustice, of the law of compensation, of unearned advantages and unrealized rewards: "The only weapon . . . that Nature seems to recognize is the boomerang,"[117] said William George Jordan. It does come back. "Nature keeps her books admirably; she puts down every item, she closes all accounts . . ."[117] She does not always seem to balance them at the end of each moment but "no man in the world ever attempted to wrong another without being injured in return — some way, somehow, sometime. . . . The most subtle of all temptations is the seeming success of the wicked. It requires moral courage to see, without flinching, material prosperity coming to men who are dishonest; to see [people] . . . rise into prominence, and power . . . by trickery and corruption."[117]

But there is a personal inner peace that comes with faith in an overruling Providence that balances accounts.

Then consider for example, "The student who becomes expert in the various devices by which the drudgery of learning is evaded [and] imagines that he is outwitting his instructors, but discovers in later life that he is cheating *himself*. The discipline of education is not the attempt of the school . . . to beneft itself. It is for . . . helping the student."[118]

The laws of health and happiness are not given just to keep us from indulging our inclinations

and appetites. They are given to keep us from
ill health and unhappiness. The commandments
are not given for the satisfaction of a Father
who likes to say thou shalt not. They are simply
a statement of cause and effect — of what will
happen *if* we do or don't do differently — for
we realize the results of the way we live life,
in this world or out of it. It comes down to
something Shakespeare said so remarkably well,
as he said so many things so remarkably well:
"Heaven is above all yet; there sits a judge that
no king can corrupt."[119]

It is wonderfully reassuring to know that there
is a system of keeping accounts that no conniv-
ance can corrupt. "The only weapon . . . that
Nature seems to recognize is the boomerang."
It does come back!

> *"No man can climb out be-*
> *yond the limitations of his own*
> *character."*
>
> —JOHN MORLEY

PART 11

> "Cultivate only the habits that you are willing should master you."
>
> —ELBERT HUBBARD

The habits we have . . .

There is this from Samuel Johnson on habit and human behavior: "The chains of habit are generally too small to be felt, until they are too strong to be broken."[120] "Do not begin," said John Locke, "to make any thing *customary*, . . . [that] you would not have continue and increase. . . ."[121]

Habits and appetites will take hold upon our lives if we let them, until they all but occupy us. "For first cometh to the mind the simple suggestion," said Thomas à Kempis, "then the strong imagination, afterwards pleasure, evil affection, assent. And so little by little the enemy entereth in altogether, because he was not resisted at the beginning."[122]

> Check the beginning:
> Once thou might'st have cured,
> But now 'tis past thy skill,
> Too long hath it endured.[122]

At some point it becomes a question of whether or not we can change our habits or feel helpless before them. To be a reasoning, responsible person we have to be alert, with fullest possible functioning both of mind and of body for the quick and complex decisions we have so many times to make. Especially should we avoid whatever would dull our senses, slow down our reactions, or interfere with our best judgment.

Call it morality, call it common sense, call it respect — respect for life, respect for others, respect for self — call it what you will — but anything that contributes to dependability, to morality, to acuteness, to self-control, to health and happiness is *good*.

Anything that slows down judgment, that dulls the senses, that increases dependence, that reduces self-control, anything that increases accidents or ill health *isn't* good.

"The habits of time," said George Cheever, "are the soul's dress for eternity"[123] and even if we have an unwise, unwholesome habit, we should not give up the honest, prayerful, continuing effort to conquer the habit we have. "Little by little, through patience and longsuffering, thou shalt conquer by the help of God, . . ."[122] A man ought to examine his habits before they become the master of the man.

Abstinence and moderation . . .

Some further words from Samuel Johnson from some two centuries ago: "Abstinence is as easy to me," he said, "as temperance would be difficult."[124]

Moderation is a word that has a very acceptable sound, and we might fall into the fallacy of thinking it is the answer to everything. But it isn't always. Indeed, there isn't anything that is always the answer to everything, and this in itself is a matter of moderation. But Samuel

Johnson's short sentence suggests that sometimes it is easier to do what seems more difficult to do than it is to do something that at first sight seems easier — for if we give up something only partly, there is always the question when, how much, how far. But if we give something up altogether, this question resolves itself. It isn't possible to sample all things and still preserve principle It isn't possible to partake of a little of everything and still preserve health — or life. Even a little of some things is too much — sometimes fatally so. Some things are wrong in any amount, basically and inherently wrong — even in moderation. We sometimes hear talk of "tapering off." It has a tempting sound. But would we recommend tapering off stealing, tapering off immorality, or tapering off something that could dishonor or destroy us — or many other things that might be mentioned?

There are often extenuating circumstances, and we cannot expect perfection, but we are stronger and safer if we face facts and not accommodate ourselves to error or evil or unhealthful habits — not even in moderation. If we have a habit which will likely lead to a wrong result, we could be safer to give it up altogether than to give it up part way.

We do ourselves a disservice if we say that a little of everything is all right, when a little of some things is really wrong. In other words, the best way not to do what we shouldn't do is not to do it. To cite again the words of Samuel Johnson: "Abstinence is as easy to me as temperance would be difficult."

Manners from models . . .

In commenting on the character and courtesy — or lack of it — of young people, of all people, Frederick K. Stamm asked: "Are the young to blame for their discourteous actions? . . . There are ways of training the youth to be . . . pleasing, and useful citizens. It can be done by parents being courteous themselves, not from a mere desire to observe convention but respect for the other members of the family as personalities. The boy will learn courtesy when he sees his father treat the boy's mother like a queen, and the wise and well-balanced girl is she whose mother maintains grace and dignity in relationships with her husband and sons."[125]

Manners, kindness, courtesy — these don't just happen. They come from several sources. "Where the spirit of love and duty pervades the home . . . where the daily life is honest and virtuous . . . kind, and loving, then may we expect . . . healthy, useful, and happy beings, . . . Models are, therefore, of every importance in moulding the nature of the child; . . . In the face of bad example, the best of precepts are of but little avail. . . . Indeed, precept at variance with practise is worse than useless . . . [for] children are judges of consistency, and the lessons of the parent who says one thing and does the opposite are quickly seen through. . . . The tiniest bits of opinion sown in the minds of children in private life afterwards issue forth to the world, and become its public opinion; for *nations are gathered out of nurseries.* . . . The manners of society at large are but the reflex of the maners of our collective homes, . . ."[126]

"Indeed, we can always better understand and appreciate a man's real character . . . [not so much] by his public exhibition of himself but by the manner in which he conducts himself towards those who are the most nearly related to him, and by his transaction of the common-place details of daily duty."[127]

Hurting ourselves . . . and others . . .

There are two unacceptable assumptions: the assumption that we can hurt ourselves without hurting others; and the assumption that we can hurt others without hurting ourselves. The words of John Muir come to mind: "When we try to pick out anything by itself, we find it hitched to everything else in the universe."[128] We are all of us interrelated. Young people cannot hurt themselves without hurting parents and all the people they are part of. We all carry around with us the reputation — the interests — of others as well as our own — of family and friends, community and country.

The success of children is the success of parents. The sorrow of children is the sorrow of parents.

If a person partakes of things that impair his physical or mental capacity, he loses in some degree what he could have been, what he could have done, and the world loses — and his loved ones lose.

If by some wrong or foolish choice, some indifference to facts, some wilful ignoring of law — the laws of health, the laws of life — if by this someone becomes ill or injured or impaired in capacity, others must care for him. If a life is prematurely lost, or lessened, the world is less. Some centuries ago, John Donne summarized in some moving, sobering words that have been much sung and said: "No man is an island, entire of itself; . . . Any man's death diminishes me, because I am involved in mankind. And therefore never send to know for whom the bell tolls; it tolls for thee."[129]

We canot hurt ourselves without hurting others. We cannot hurt others without hurting ourselves. This, young people — indeed all of us — would well remember — for, in success or sorrow, families, friends, loved ones belong to each other — and if we hurt ourselves of misuse our lives, the hurt carries over to others also. "No man is an island."

On making memories . . .

In this marvelous mind, this marvelous memory God has given (infinitely beyond the capacity that anyone has ever reached or realized) are stored away the impressions of life: what we have done and seen and thought and heard and said — all that makes the total experience of each of us.

Sometimes thoughts come quickly when we want to recall them. Sometimes it takes a moment, or less or longer, to remember what we would like to remember. Sometimes memories, impressions, come to our consciousness uninvited, whether we wish them to or not.

The working and the wonder of it all, no man is wise enough to know. But one of the sobering lessons of life is this: the record is there — thoughts, experiences, impressions of places and people — all of them — and the *unwanted* thoughts return as well as *wanted* ones — the negative, the unclean stories, the sordid sights and scenes, as well as wholesome, pleasant, happy sights and scenes. And so the responsibility of making memories, for ourselves and others, is with us always.

This places upon parents the sacred obligation to help make people happy, with wholesome memories for children; happy memories of home. It places upon teachers, upon us all, the duty to deal with them in fairness, kindness, encouragement; with memories that will bless and strengthen and sustain them later in life. This places upon us all the obligation to deal with all others in honor — always, wherever we are, to live and act and be so as not to be embarrassed when we meet any person, any place, when memories choose to return: to live so as far as possible, to remember happily the whole life, and to help make that kind of memories for others also.

Everyone who deals with anyone in the closest or in the most remote relationships of life should so live as to make memories pleasant, honorable, righteous, fair — so as not to be embarrassed to meet anyone, anywhere. As memory brings back its pictures and impressions we should remember to *do* what we will be happy to remember *we have done.*

"Our deeds still travel with us from afar, And what we have been makes us what we are."

—George Eliot

PART 12

> "Unless the vessel is clean, whatever you pour into it turns sour."
>
> —Horace

"I had a pleasant time with my mind . . ."

There is a thoughtful line from Louisa May Alcott: "I had a pleasant time with my mind, for it was happy."[130] The mind, of course, can go anywhere, even when the body is infirm or confined. Consciously or subconsciously the mind is always in motion. And it is still true that as a man thinketh, so is he.[131]

"If you keep your mind sufficiently open," one observer said, "people will throw a lot of rubbish into it."[132] They will, and they do, if we let them. And it is for us to see that we select wholesome, mental fare for ourselves in what we read and see and hear, and also concern ourselves with what is taught our children by all means by which impressions are made upon their minds — for what moves in our minds is the pattern of what will come to pass unless something prevents.

It is in the mind that music and poetry are first fashioned. It is in the mind that envy and evil are incubated, that crime is first committed, that morality and immorality are made. And in the mind beauty and good are born. In the mind our future is made, and we *are* responsible for the thoughts we think and for the purposes we pursue.

There is nothing we know of more marvellous than the human mind, except the infinite mind of God who gave it. And one cannot conceive of anyone's using any drug or dope or mind-dulling substance that would impair the senses, or interfere with judgment or self-control, or any way mar the mind of man — this great and sensitive instrument that God has given.

If we are clean in mind, we are clean and happy in life. If we are evil in mind, we are not happy anywhere. "Clean up your thought," said Dr. Frank Crane. "Don't have a waste - basket mind."[133] God give us the wisdom to respect our minds, and not clutter them with trash or trivia or unwholesome content of any kind — for the mind in large measure is where we live our lives.

"Let virtue garnish thy thoughts unceasingly; *then* shall thy confidence wax strong in the presence of God."[134] "I had a pleasant time with my mind, for it was happy."

Clean - what a wonderful word . . .

There is a word that has within it some wonderful possibilties for personal peace, for safety, for self-respect, and the word is called "clean." Clean hands, clean hearts, clean homes; clean waters, clean air, clean clothes — clean minds, clean morals — what a wonderful word!

The mind so often follows environment — and the cycle reverses itself, as environment follows the mind. We can have a hopeful outlook in almost anything, if we commit ourselves to cleanliness, to being clean.

"There is a beauty every girl has —" said David O. McKay, "a gift from God, as pure as the sunlight, and as sacred as life. It is a beauty all men love, a virtue that wins all men's souls. That beauty is chastity. A beautiful, modest chaste woman is creation's masterpiece."[135] "Walk in the spirit," said Paul, "and ye shall not fulfil the lust of the flesh. . . . the fruit of the Spirit is love, joy, peace, longsuffering, gentleness, goodness, faith, ..."[136] "Let our thoughts, words, dress and general deportment indicate our belief in the sanctity of the body as the temple of God," said Hugh B. Brown, "even as Paul declared it to be:[137] 'Wherefore come out from among [the world] . . . and touch not the unclean thing; and I will receive you, and will be a Father unto you, and ye shall be my sons and daughters. . . .' "[138]

Evil isn't clean. Evil keeps company with unclean minds, unclean morals, unclean attitudes, unclean atmosphere. That "cleanliness is next to godliness" is not just an old adage but a real fact to face: cleanliness of thought, of person, of dress, of speech. There is not only "the strength of being clean," but peace and safety and self-respect.

Youth can reach the highest of the heights if youth will commit itself to being clean. "How glorious and near to the angels is youth that is clean."[139] God help us to commit ourselves to cleanliness.

The humor that makes us ashamed

There is a searching, meaningful sentence from Emerson:

"Beware of jokes . . . [from which] we go away hollow and ashamed."[140] This is the humor that hurts, the humor that plays on adverse personal attributes, and embarrasses the defenseless subject, publicly or privately. But there is to be considered also the humor that debases, the crude, low-minded humor, the essence of which is immoral suggestion: making light of lewdness, making light of marital unfaithfulness, of human depravity, or of evil obscenities.

"The manner of jesting ought not to be extravagant or immoderate, but refined and witty . . ." said Cicero. "There are, generally speaking, two sorts of jests: the one, coarse, rude, vicious, indecent; the other polite, refined, clever, witty [which], if well timed, is becoming to the most dignified person. The other," he said, "is unfit for any gentleman."[141]

It has been said that a civilization could be judged by its humor — and what can be said of a civilization could also be said in part of people personally. When any man makes humor out of human depravity or baseness, lewd suggestion, or immoral action, one may reasonably suppose that at least his judgment is at fault, and that maybe his mind runs low.

Heaven help us never to lose our sense of humor. But heaven help us also to avoid the humor that is based on ridicule or embarrassing physical factors, or the humor that is based on unclean suggestion or low-minded morals. "Beware of jokes . . . [from which] we go away hollow and ashamed."

If we patronize evil . . .

With increasing concern for the lowering standards of morality and decency, there comes the question what to do about it? Should we just sit in resignation as if we were watching the progress of a play — or is there something we can do to change the trend?

One hopeful aspect of it is the growing determination on the part of many responsible people, publicly and privately, to draw a line against looseness and lawlessness. But in some ways there is still indifference or discouragement as to altering the outcome. And it would seem to be far past time to face some very simple facts — and one of them is this: Part of the reason why evil is possible is because it is made to be profitable. Another fact: We may be against it in principle, and still patronize it, and make it further possible by making it further profitable.

This applies to any form of evil that is offered to the public as a marketable product. If we patronize or partake of any thing that isn't good for people, we are helping to expand it by helping to make it profitable. If, for any reason whatsoever, we purchase or procure any of the salacious products of pornography, in picture or in print, we help to make this evil profitable. If we patronize a lewd or raw or immoral play, by whatever means it is presented or produced — if we put our money down to see something filthy and immoral — we are not only degrading ourselves, but we are helping to promote and proliferate such productions by making them profitable.

Evil is greedy. Evil is pursued by many to make money. And always we ought to remember that the more profitable evil is, the more powerful it is, and the more prevalent it will become.

Evil will go just as far as we let it. If we patronize it, encourage it, it will go to unlimited lengths. But we personally can play an important part by not patronizing, not purchasing, not making profitable anything of evil or of low-minded morals. If something isn't good for people, it doesn't matter how profitable or popular or prevalent it is, we ought to leave it alone.

Act well thy part

An inscription over a Scottish doorway, had this to say: "What e'er thou art, act well thy part."[25] This ties somewhat to the scripture that says: "Abstain from all appearance of evil."[142] If negative appearance is evil, positive appearance must be good.

Behavioral studies suggest that when people of eccentric habit and unclean person are cleaned and groomed and respectably dressed, many become responsible and compatible and well performing people. An actor feels and sometimes lives the part he plays — and so, to a degree, do all of us, and there is cause to be concerned about the part people choose to play, the appearance they choose to present, the company they choose to keep.

We expect professional people to look like what they are. We expect a doctor to have dignity, confidence, composure. We expect teachers to appear and be at their best, with decorum and good taste; students to be clean and respectfully attired, avoiding extremes; parents to appear in good taste and dignity before the family, and children likewise in self-respect and respect for others, in cleanliness with family and friends.

Appearing the part is more than a front. It is part of being the part. A careless and unclean person is likely to feel careless and unclean; and so it is with immodesty and other aspects also.

Appearance is both a symptom and a source, and the side effects are exceedingly significant. Appearance also plays a vital part in the reaction of others to us. And so we should appear as we ought to be, and be what we ought to be, improve our part, our personality, our performance, upgrade ourselves and our surroundings, and not let ourselves slip in appearance, or thought, or attitude or action. As we appear, our influence and example will affect others — and us. "What e'er thou art, act well thy part."

"By nothing do men show their character more than by the things they laugh at."

—Goethe

PART 13

"The more weakness, the more falsehood; strength goes straight."

—Jean Paul Richter

"Don't ever take a fence down . . . until . . ."

Don't ever take a fence down," said G. K. Chesterton, "until you know the reason it was put up."[143] Too many people in too many places tend to remove time-honored safeguards, the reasons for which they do not know.

Change is inevitable; fashions will be made and unmade as far as we can foresee. But there are extremists and exhibitionists who flagrantly defy standards, principles, law, morals, modesty.

There is, among other things, good taste to be considered. As Alexander Pope said it: "Be not the first by whom the new are tried, nor yet the last to lay the old aside."[144] But the crux is the difference between what is a principle and what is merely a preference.

There are some foundations that are firmly fixed. If not, there is nothing that one can measure by or count on, except his own preference, his own mood of the moment, and that, of course, is chaos. There are some foundational principles, some standards, some basic qualities of character without which there is no progress, no asurance, without which no society or no person is safe: Honesty, morality, respect for law — such things don't go out of force even if, with some, they seem to go out of fashion. It is so easy to tear down; so easy to reject, so easy to discredit, but the commandments are still there. Cause and consequences are still there, and if we tamper irresponsibly, ignorantly, or even innocently, with the basic laws of life, we shall find to our sorrow why the fence was put up in the first place.

As to modesty, morality, chastity, honesty and honor, one cannot break from the basic foundations and have assurance for the future. Paul said it in a strong, short sentence: "Let all things be done decently, and in order."[145] Don't ever take a fence down until you know the reason why it was put up."

... until it was tested ...

There is an interesting observation from a person who acquired some equipment, which looked good until he tried to use it for the purpose for which it was purchased — and then it wouldn't work. "The failure," he said, "was discovered only when it was required to perform."[146] That is a very incisive sentence. In other words, it looked good — until it was tested.

Many theories look good until they are tested. Many people look good until they are tested. Many seem trustworthy until they are tested. Every borrower promises to pay. With every bride and groom there is an implied promise of faithfulness, love, and loyalty. People, principles, philosophies, theories, beliefs, convictions, all promise, in a sense, to solve problems, to stand the test. But then comes the testing time: accidents, illness, old age, death, the loss of a loved one; unhappiness, depression, some tragedy, some trouble, some temptation — and then we find how workable or unworkable they are — how functional are our philosophies.

Any rope will hold when there is no weight on it — but we need to know what we can count on when the weight is heavy, when sorrows and temptations and counter purposes are pulling hard against us. We need moral and spiritual resources that will hold tight when the test comes. It is tragic to see someone carrying around a fragile philosophy that doesn't sustain him under such circumstances. And it is tragic to see those who would destroy a sustaining faith, and put nothing in its place.

"Some day, in the years to come," said Phillips Brooks, "you will be wrestling with the great temptation, or trembling under the great sorrow of your life. But the real struggle is here, now . . . *now* it is being decided whether, in the day of your supreme sorrow or temptation, you shall miserably fail or gloriously conquer. Character cannot be made except by a steady, long continued process."[6]

Thank God for the old and proved principles of faith, work, morality, industry, honesty — for principles that prove themselves when they are tested — when they are required to perform.

... If we don't have standards ...

There is a simple, forthright subject that we would turn to, namely: virtue, honor, chastity; the living of a clean and honorable life. It has to do with standards, morality, law, and even what we call commandments. Despite the inclination of anyone to minimize them, these are important to the living of a good and happy life. No one has ever proved otherwise, and the unhappiness and degradation of people personally, and the downfall of immoral, corrupt civilizations offer more proof than anyone would reasonably want.

There is another phase of this subject, and that is this: If we don't have standards, we don't know how to live life. If we don't have standards, we don't know how to judge, or choose, or measure. If we don't have standards, laws, principles, we don't know what is or isn't acceptable, and so we run loose, always in uncertainty concerning ourselves, not knowing what or where we are, or what we ought to be, or what is expected of us in the living of our lives.

How can we expect a generation to grow up happy, stable, solid, firmly directed, firmly fixed, if we don't give them standards to measure by? Once we break over or eliminate any standard or principle, any boundary, any guidelines in life — once we remove the stars, the compass, the fixed points — we have left ourselves without any way to know where we are or where we are going. And if by our misguidance, or lack of guidance, we let or encourage a generation of young people to run morally loose, we shall have lost for them the foundations of goodness and happiness, of peace and purpose, and that would be a heavy weight for anyone to carry around.

If we want happiness, here and hereafter, we must ourselves live the laws, the commandments, the principles, the standards of cleanliness, of moral conduct, of virtue, honesty, chastity — must *teach* them and *show* them these timeless and eternal truths.

Where would we be without stars, compass, standards, fixed points, guidelines in life?

We come finally to a simple, sacred, solid four-word phrase: ". . . wickedness never was happiness."[10]

On dragging others down . . .

In our concern for restlessness and lawlessness and moral looseness we need some searching of ourselves, remembering that any compromise of principle, or any letting down in example or in attitude of any parent or teacher, or anyone who influences young people, leads to a letting down of their standards of life. And anyone who lets down a little, may find that his children, or his young friends, let down further than the example they follow. And it is awesome to contemplate the responsibility of influencing the lives, the minds, the morals, the faith, the ideals of others, in leading them to lower levels.

This laxity and looseness, if unchecked, will break the hearts, the homes, the happiness of people, young and old, and lead to a kind of jungle law. Already there is evidence of the price being paid, in broken lives, in disease and shame and sorrow.

One of the "first and foremost" facts to face, to cite a current source, "is . . . that Nature is the expression of a definite order with which nothing interferes successfully, and that the chief business of men is to learn that order, and govern themselves accordingly."[147]

"The light cannot come," said Phillips Brooks, "except through purity and righteousness; lust and iniquity are surely darkness. . . . Oh, that there could thrill through the being of our young men," he added, "some electrical sense that they are God's sons, that they might . . . live the life and attain the nature which are rightly theirs."[148]

Those who would undermine the moral foundations, and who would teach youth that there are no eternal principles, no hereafter, no God-given moral law, would well remember the awesome responsibility of helping to drag anyone down.

Heaven help us all to see that youth are never led to lower moral levels — help us to lift them with the righteous influence of our lives, that truth and decency may endure as an ideal on earth — for there cannot be peace or happiness in departing from moral principles.

Some laws too seldom considered . . .

In our concern for liberty, and law, and lawlessness, and what is or isn't legal or moral or permissible, there sometimes seems to be too much complexity. The endless process of passing many laws, and the endless legal quibbling and contention suggest the need for something simpler — something too seldom considered — even something seldom if ever read or seldom heard by some — something such as the Ten Commandments. While they may not cover all the intricacies of modern life, they do provide the basic principles.

"And the Lord God came down . . . and . . . called Moses up to the top of the mountain. . . . And Moses went up unto God, and the Lord called unto him . . . saying:

> Thou shalt have no other gods before me.
>
> Thou shalt not make unto thee any graven image. . . . Thou shalt not bow down thyself to them nor serve them . . .
>
> Thou shalt not take the name of the Lord, thy God, in vain . . .
>
> Remember the sabbath day, to keep it holy.
>
> Honour thy father and thy mother: that thy days may be long upon the land which the Lord thy God giveth thee.
>
> Thou shalt not kill.
>
> Thou shalt not commit adultery.

Thou shalt not steal.

Thou shalt not bear false witness . . .

Thou shalt not covet thy neighbour's house . . . thy neighbour's wife . . . nor anything that is thy neighbour's.

"And all the people answered together, and said, all that the Lord hath spoken we will do . . . lest we die. And Moses said unto the people, fear not: for God is come to prove you, . . . that ye sin not. . . . And the Lord said . . . Ye have seen that I have talked with you from heaven."[149]

It is nowhere written, that we know of, that these principles have been repealed — but only added unto, so far as we are aware. And despite all technicalities, all attempt to dispute, to dilute, to rationalize the law, these are the commandments God has given — these — with others from the same source — which would make a good place to begin to solve our problems, to heal the heartaches, to halt the violence, to clean out the clutter of sin, and to quiet the sorrow in the lives of perplexed people. This is the way, this is the counsel God has given.

"Fear God, and keep his commandments: for this is the whole duty of man."

—OLD TESTAMENT, ECCL. 12:13

PART 14

> "No man is above the law and no man is below it; nor do we ask any man's permission when we require him to obey it."
>
> —THEODORE ROOSEVELT

Life without law

A mong the things for which we should be most grateful are commandments, standards, discipline and law. Without these there would be little that we could count on. Suppose there were no standards. Suppose that teachers, professors, academic institutions gave us no idea what was required of us to graduate or attain a degree, to qualify to practice a profession. How would we ever know what to begin to do, what to begin to be, or when we had fulfilled requirements?

Suppose that parents gave us no idea what is expected of us, but simply turned us loose to do anything, to act in any way, honest, moral, or otherwise. Suppose that God had given us no knowledge of what is expected of us — no purpose, no standards, no requirements, no commandments. What a loose and helpless life it would be not to know.

One of the greatest blessings of life is law. Without it ownership of property would not be possible. Safety would not be possible. Civilization would not be possible. Life would scarcely be possible. Poorly as it sometimes is observed, badly as it may sometimes be abused and broken, it is law basically that holds us together, that assures pay for work, title to property, protection of person. Even the lives of the lawless would be intolerable, insupportable, without law.

And so before being rebellious or abandoning commandments; before flaunting morals, destroying conventions, ridiculing responsible conduct; before disrespecting those who enforce the law; before opposing parents, teachers, those who have concern and interest in us, stop and think what life would be like without law, how little we would have without law, how little incentive there would be to produce or to learn without law.

Thank God for knowledge of what is expected of us, for parents who care enough to counsel, to discipline, to persuade; for teachers who care enough to establish and maintain standards; for a God and Father who cares enough to give us purpose, counsel, commandments. Without law, commandments, standards, discipline, we would be utterly loose and utterly lost.

. . . for lessons we refuse to learn . . .

Life is good —if we will live to let it be. It is also difficult at times. No one ever said it wouldn't be. Certainly the Father of us all did not say so. But, as a loving Father, He has given us counsel and precautions, and has "warned and forewarned" us according to His own words. In a sense, He says to us: Don't clutter up your life with things that are sure to damage the mind, distress the spirit, which are sure to destroy health and peace, and embarrass and disquiet conscience, and cause a complexity of personal problems.

Some things are good for man. Some things are not good for man. This is true morally, physically, spiritually. And yet with all the experience of the ages, and all the counsel God has given, we keep repeating many of the same mistakes — in a sense, hitting our heads against a wall, perhaps wondering why the wall remains while our heads are hurting. It comes down to a question of listening to counsel, learning the commandments and keeping them.

". . . The hour will be a priceless one," wrote Lida Churchill, "in which one faces the truth, for it is a truth, and a most important one, that no one is free in the sense in which the unthinking mind regards freedom."[150] It is true that we are free to choose, but we are not free from the consequences that come from choosing. We are not free from the operation of the law.

"To be deceived by our enemies or betrayed by our friends is insupportable;" said a French philosopher, "yet to be deceived by ourselves is worse . . ."[151] The Creator knows what will bring happiness and misery to man, and we should not deceive ourselves that we can do anything that is not good for people, or for us personally, without paying a price.

"There is a law . . ." — a law of health, a law of happiness, a law of peace and progress — "upon which all blessings are predicated"[152] —

and we cannot safely set aside what has been tested and proven over and over in the past, without paying a personal price for each lesson we refuse to learn.

"A new crop of fools comes on . . ."

This message was once sent to a president of the United States by a group of concerned young people: "We stand for preservation of our heritage through obedience to law."[153]

Without law, respect for it, living by it, upholding it, we would have no heritage. Law sustains life. Law keeps the universe in its course. Law assures that orderly processes will lead to known results. Without law there would be no safety, no standards, no assurance, no guidelines in life. Without law men, nature, life, would be in complete chaos. Then why, Oh why should there be looseness pertaining to law, failure to uphold it.

Frank Crane once gave some terse sentences on this subject: "Every generation a new crop of fools comes on," he said. "They think they can beat the orderly universe. They conceive themselves to be more clever than the eternal laws. They snatch goods from Nature's store, and run. . . . And one by one they all come back to Nature's counter, and pay — pay in tears, in agony, in despair; pay as fools before them have paid. . . . Nature keeps books pitilessly. Your credit with her is good, but she collects; there is no land you can flee to and escape her bailiffs. . . . She never forgets; she sees to it that you pay her every cent you owe, with interest."[154]

Thank God for law, for those who respect it, live by it, help to sustain it: for the laws of health; for the renewal of the air and water of the earth — for seeds that produce what was planted, for the succession of the seasons, for everything that leads to a known result, and sustains life, and makes peace and orderly purpose possible.

Everything we have, everything we may ever expect to have, everything we can count on would be lacking without law. Everything that we *can* count on comes with living and working with law. "We stand for the preservation of our heritage through obedience to law."

The laws and constitution of our country

There is need to retell from time to time the principles on which freedom is founded, and which continue to make it rare among men. If we don't re-tell it to our children — and to ourselves — it will be less and less understood — or even lost.

"There is . . . an . . . inclination," said General Harbord, "to feel deep down inside ourselves that our blessings 'just happen' . . . but the condition upon which God has given liberty to man is eternal vigilance." ". . . every citizen should remember that liberty . . . did not just 'come to pass.'[155] It has been won, step by step — and dearly won — through the centuries. It can be lost — and dearly lost — in a fraction of the time [it took] to build it. It can slip away through unnoticed infringements . . . If great numbers of our citizens cease to believe deeply in individual liberty, tolerance, self-respect; . . . cease to thrill with thankfulness for the inestimable freedoms they enjoy we may lose these priceless privileges — even as citizens of other nations have."[156]

And so we reaffirm our faith in the Constitution of our country ". . . a glorious standard; . . . a heavenly banner; . . . founded in the wisdom of God,"[157] — "by the hands of wise men whom [He] raised up unto this very purpose,"[158] to make possible the full free living of life — and it is still the bulwark of freedom among men.

We didn't do all this ourselves. But the price of enjoying the privileges is the price of accepting the responsibilities — both personal and public — with understanding, with temperance, with liberty and respect for law, and with an awareness "that freedom and responsibility are inseparable."[159]

"The laws and constitution of the people . . . should be maintained for the rights and protection of all flesh, according to just and holy principles; that every man may act . . . according to the moral agency . . . given unto him, that every man may be accountable for his own sins in the day of judgment."[160] We reaffirm our faith in the Constitution of our country. And may we never see it silently whittled away or interpreted out of intent.

. . . *the character of our country* . . .

S ome historians say there have been some nineteen civilizations rise and fall in human history, and the principal cause for downfall was moral decay. Civilization and survival, are, besides all else, matters of morals. If we have no sound moral foundation, we have no safety, no assurance for the future.

"Let us," said Charles Sumner, "turn our thoughts on the character of our country."[161] Let us instil in youth, decency, honesty, cleanliness in conduct. Let homes, parents, teachers, textbooks, entertainment and all else that is offered them — all that goes to make the man — be shaped and fashioned in truth and dignity and decency — so shaped that they can and will sincerely say "On my honor, I will do my best — To do my duty to God and my Country, . . ."[162] — to keep the commandments. Except it be so, we shall find that what we are sowing will rot as it ripens.

". . . there is even now something of ill omen amongst us," said Abraham Lincoln. "I mean the increasing disregard for law . . . the growing disposition to substitute the wild and furious passions in lieu of the sober judgment of courts, . . ."[163] "The world no longer has a choice between force and law;" said Dwight Eisenhower, "If civilization is to survive it must choose the rule of law."[164]

"At what point then is the approach of danger to be expected?" Lincoln continued. "I answer, If it ever reach us it must spring up amongst us; . . . If destruction be our lot we must ourselves be its author and finisher. As a nation of freemen, we must live through all time or die by suicide."[163]

What then shall we say for the future — what shall we say of what some would call this twentieth civilization? It comes down, finally, to a question of character — the character of each of us — "the character of our country." "We — even we here — hold the power and bear the responsibility. . . . We shall nobly save or meanly lose the last, best hope of earth."[165]

"True liberty consists in the privilege of enjoying our own rights, not in the destruction of the rights of others."

—GEORGE PINCKARD

PART 15

"*The happier the time, the more quickly it passes.*"

—Pliny the Younger

MOTHER'S DAY

Oh! be there, mothers - be there . . .

Some time ago I found two pigeons making a crude nest in a secluded crevice outside one of my windows. It was winter. It was cold. Food must have been difficult to find. It was the mother who stayed. It was the mother who stood her ground against my close approaches. It was the mother who kept watch and warmth against all elements until her two young birds were safely out of their shells. It was the mother who somehow found food and fed them, until they were able to fly for themselves. It was the mother who was there, and won my utmost respect for her unfailing performance. Oh, what admiration for those creatures that faithfully follow the mother instinct in them!

In many ways it has been the mothers of all times — everywhere — who have been there when needed — as needed — always. How wonderful to find a mother waiting — watching — being there — as children come home and ask, "Where is mother?" — mothers who mold the personality, who set the cast of character, who guide and shape the future — who make home a place of peace, of pleasantness: who listen, share, set standards, give counsel and encouragement, and give children an awareness they are wanted. Mothers are the heart of the home: humble, faithful, modest mothers — loving, serving, quietly teaching — virtue, honor, honesty, keeping promises; understanding mistakes; doing the duties of each day with love and unselfishness in giving of themselves. A mother at home, a mother waiting, is one of the greatest sources of safety and assurance. And returning to an empty home — or house — leaves so much lacking. "Is mother at home?" "Where is mother?"

Oh, be there, mothers — be there — for your presence will bless your children now, and always —and forever. Oh, be there. God bless mothers and their memories.

MEMORIAL DAY

"All day we miss thee, everywhere"

Never too far from our thoughts are questions concerning the length of life, the purpose of life — life, death, loss of loved ones, the whereabouts of those who leave us, and our own time of leaving those we love. These are among the most insistent questions of all time.

As to those we have lost, those we may lose, and as to ourselves: "No cogent reason remains for supposing the soul dies with the body. . . ."

said Dr. Arthur H. Compton. "We (scientists) find strong reasons for believing that man is of extraordinary importance in the cosmic scheme. . . . It takes a lifetime to build the character of a noble man. The exercise and discipline of youth, the struggles and failures of maturity, the loneliness and tranquility of age — these make the fire through which he must pass to bring out the pure gold of his soul. Having been thus perfected, what shall Nature do with him, annihilate him? What infinite waste! As long as there is in heaven a God of love there must be for God's children *everlasting life!*[166] So spoke this eminent scientist whose knowledge was full of reason and whose reason was full of faith.

All of us have losses — or will have — and no matter how many friends we have, or family, the loss of one beloved loved one leaves always a place unfilled in our hearts, as David Macbeth Moir said it:

> We miss thy small step on the stair;
> We miss thee at thine evening prayer;
> All day we miss thee, everywhere.[167]

To you who know the loss of loved ones, to you who think upon your own time — sometime — of leaving this life: there *is* a place where loved ones wait, a place, a purpose, and an everlastingness of life in the real and substantive sense.

God grant to each one faith and peace and purpose, and memories made sweeter by this assurance, that when we go it will not be as strangers, but to find again beloved faces, the personal presence of family and friends.

FATHER'S DAY

Fathers: example and imitation

We turn a moment to what could be called an item on imitation, going back some years to something Carl Van Doren said — that ". . . small boys instinctively mimic their fathers . . . [This is] part of every boy's education . . . little boys . . . hurrying to keep up with longer legs . . . in imitation and admiration. A small boy then will give up almost any play to imitate his father at work. He asks endless questions, in the serene assurance that his father will know the answers."

But after "this age of imitation and admiration" there may come periods of questioning, of "disagreement," periods of "independence." Then with more maturity, such differences tend to disappear, as the hearts of fathers and sons humbly turn toward each other, with appreciation and respect. The sons have children, and come to discover that "life is a good deal like father said."

Finally comes the loss of a father, and a son feels the "loneliness" that comes with the loss of strength and love on which he had learned to lean; then more and more sons feel themselves as fathers and turn more dearly to their own children.[168] This cycle suggests some sober searching.

Our Lord and Savior said: "The Son can do nothing of himself, but what he seeth the Father do."[169] He also said: "Be ye therefore perfect, even as your Father which is in heaven is perfect. . . ."[170] Again the example and imitation, with a heavy weight of responsibility — a weight that fathers carry always concerning their children. And in looking for solutions to problems we sometimes look a generation too late, for example and imitation are sometimes at the source. As Samuel Eliot said: "The influence of a man is not just in what he says [or does] but what he is. Character is singularly contagious."[171]

There is the further sobering fact that when we choose to marry, we choose, in effect, someone whom our children are likely to imitate, someone whose beliefs, convictions, and character we would want them to follow — or so choose we should.

Thank God for the love and confidence and companionship of fathers, for respect and understanding, always with an awareness of example and imitation — for fathers whose names we bear, whose heritage we have, whose footsteps we may follow, with respect, along with love.

THANKSGIVING

. . . for life . . . for law
. . . for loved ones . . .

So much we have to be grateful for, that almost it overwhelms us, almost before we begin. And among the blessings God has given are life, and law, and loved ones. Without law, there would be no assurance that a man could enjoy the fruits of his labors. Without law, commandments, standards, there would be nothing to measure by — no way to know what is expected of us — nothing to live up to — little that we could count on. Without law, ownership of property would not be possible. Safety would not be possible. Civilization would not be possible. What a loose and helpless life it would be without law. And, indeed, in the ultimate, without law there would be no life.

Along with thankfulness for law, thanks for loved ones, for friends; for food, for water, for air; for the sea, the stars, the seasons; seeds that grow; the beauty of the earth — for the wonder of it all; for mother, father, family — for the laughter of children, the wondering innocence of their eyes; for the trusting hand of a child.

Thanks for warmth, for sleep, for sunrise; music; mountains, fields, forests. Thanks for work, for education, opportunity; for those who make employment possible.

Thanks for just being alive, — and for the assurance that God lives, that life has meaning and eternal purpose — that life is everlasting, that loved ones live even after they have left us — that the renewal of association with loved ones is part of our Father's purpose and plan. Thanks for a Savior who taught us of life, and redeemd us from death.

"God's goodness hath been great to thee,"[172] said Shakespeare. "Should not this great goodness," said William Penn, "raise a due sense in us of . . . resolution to alter our course and mend our manners."[173]

Life, law, loved ones — thanks for all of this, and much more. "Let never day or night unhallowed pass, But still remember what the Lord hath done."[172]

CHRISTMAS

Christmas - and memories to your children

At Christmas there is so much intermingled — children — innocence, expectancy; loved ones — homecoming, happiness, gay and mellow moods; sometimes loneliness — serious concerns; generosity in some measure, and some emerging of our better selves — and so much else besides — all intermixed with a measure of forgiving and forgetting — and with memories from all past years that merge and mingle with the present moment.

Oh, parents, we would plead, give good and happy memories to your children — not pampering or overindulging, not satisfying everything they take a fancy to — but memories of love, encouragement, of peace and harmony and happiness at home — memories that will bless and lift their lives wherever they are, always and forever.

Well, swiftly now it comes and goes, and so does life. Oh, let us live it with repentance and improvement, with honesty and honor, and with a balance of mind and heart and spirit — along with all the tangibles that are so much in evidence.

And one could not, of course, conceive of Christmas without Him whose coming it commemorates: the Prince of Peace, the Son of God, our Saviour and Redeemer, concerning whom we witness that He lives, from deep within the certainty of our souls. "I know that my Redeemer liveth."

Oh, may we not forget at any time what God has given, or overemphasize the troubles of our time, but go with patience, gratitude and faith into the future, remembering from Longfellow these hopeful, moving lines:

> I heard the bells on Christmas day
> Their old familiar carols play;
> And wild and sweet the words repeat
> Of peace on earth, good will to men.
>
> And in despair I bowed my head:
> "There is no peace on earth," I said
> For hate is strong and mocks the song
> Of peace on earth, good will to men."
>
> Then pealed the bells more loud and deep:
> "God is not dead, nor doth he sleep;
> The wrong shall fail the right prevail,
> With peace on earth, good will to men."[174]

> *"Goe, and catche a falling*
> *starre, . . .*
> *Tell me, where all past yeares*
> *are, . . ."*
>
> —JOHN DONNE

PART 16

"The fool, with all his other faults, has this also: he is always getting ready to live."

—Epicurus

"My departed hours - where are they?"

"My departed hours—where are they?"[175]— the poet asked in anguish. The weeks seem hours only. And when we look at what we do with days, the lost times, the in-between times, we wonder at the time we waste away — sometimes looking at or listening to what isn't worth the time it takes; sometimes reading what isn't worth the time it takes; sometimes reading what isn't worth the paper it is printed on; sometimes thoughts that never should have been thought or written.

"What is time?" asked Longfellow. "The shadow on the dial, the striking of the clock, the running of the sand . . . ? These are but . . . outward signs , . . . Time is the Life of the soul."[176] Time, life, choice: — the very essence of all we are or shall be — ever.

And mayhap we ought to make our own time-and-motion studies in our own personal pursuits, and note the difference between going forward and merely going through motions; and not so much needlessly do the same things over and over again: such as sometimes shifting and re-shuffling the same pile of papers and putting them in different places, without really clearing up the clutter; sometimes doing essentially the same with problems — worrying and re-worrying about the same ones without doing what can or should be done; sometimes wrestling with the same habits, the same appetites, the same troubled conscience, without really repenting or improving or really learning our lessons.

With time moving, chimes sounding, life passing, just going through motions is not enough. There are some things we ought to be doing now, or ought already to have done. Oh, may we have the wisdom to use the little time, the precious life, to do what should be done, to learn what should be learned, to live as we should live: repenting, improving, performing, with a blessed sense of peace and purpose — not just rearranging our problems — not just rushing around.

"... emphatic trifles ..."

The swift passing of a season is always sobering — for "Time," said Benjamin Franklin, "is the stuff life is made of."[177] And while time in the eternal sense is limitless, what we can now foresee passes swiftly. And yet we often splinter it away with less thought, less purpose, less accomplishment than time is entitled to.

"At times," said Emerson, "the whole world seems to be in conspiracy to importune you with emphatic trifles."[178] It is true that other people splinter our lives into trifles if we let them, and often we ourselves do the same. Often we let our lives be cluttered with encumbrances — with bits and pieces and paraphernalia — with "emphatic trifles" as Emerson said. And while we don't want to be slaves to unreasoning routine, we ought to recognize the waste when time is not well used — for "Time," said Diogenes, "is the most valuable thing that a man can spend."[179]

"Don't waste time," pleaded Arthur Brisbane, "Don't waste it in idleness; don't waste it in regretting the time already wasted; don't waste it in dissipation; don't waste it in resolutions a thousand times repeated, never to be carried out. Don't waste your time. Use all of it. Sleep, work, rest, think. Save part of the time of yesterday by saving part of the money earned yesterday. . . . The best of us have already wasted time enough. . . . Remember that however much time you have wasted already, you have time enough left [for some accomplishment and recovery] if you will use it . . . while life and time remain."[180]

Passing and trivial things should not be allowed unduly to take us away from more productive pursuits, nor should we let others often distract us with trifles that take us away from our work. "At times the whole world seems to be in conspiracy to importune you with emphatic trifles."

Now make the most of it!

S omewhere the story is told of a talented girl who seemed not to be doing enough with the gifts and abilities that she had been given, and under some urgent impulse her mother one day impatiently shook her and, in substance, said: "I've given you life. Now you do something with it!"

We could conceive of the Father of us all saying about the same: "I've given you life. Now make the most of it!" I've given you time, opportunity, talent, intelligence, the good earth and all it offers — now use it, do something with it! This brings to mind a line, not often heard or said these days, but much full of meaning: "We are not here to play, to dream, to drift."

One of the most wasteful wastes in the world is the waste of time, of talent, of opportunity, of creative effort, — indifference to development, indifference to learning, indifference to work — the don't-care, drop-out, what's-the-use attitude.

There are times for preparation, and times for serious, responsible performance, and we had better be finding direction, finding ourselves, and moving forward, avoiding indifferent drifting or wasteful delay in using the priceless abilities and opportunities God has given.

One of the steadying factors in this broad and blessed land, and in each one's life — one that would reduce restlessness and discontent — would be for all of us to make commitment to use in more useful ways the best of our abilities, perhaps with a sense that the Father of us all might somehow, sometime shake us, and unforgettably say (which He has, in more ways than we seem to be aware): "I have given you life. Now, make the most of it!"

. . . and even forgive ourselves . . .

All of us are aware at times of fretfulness and frustration — and are sometimes troubled, discouraged, discontent, as we lose the peace, the sense of purpose, that are always so essential to an inner calm and quiet. And these frustrations are added unto as we see days swiftly slip away, and see ourselves running, going, coming, using up the hours, not doing all we should, and, in our efforts to catch up and to recover, wavering with excesses, with upswings and downswings; high in spirit at times, depressed at others; so much undone and so much that is overdone.

And so, with some self-searching, we would plead for calm and quiet, for patience, contemplation, and for reappraisal of our purpose, with faith in the limitless and everlasting possibilities of life.

And, along with faith, we need repentance, understanding, charity, forgiveness, as all of us come face to face with an appraisal of our past, with the uses of the present, and a turning to the values that will last the longest.

And let us, please God, learn the uselessness of enmity — enmity toward evil, yes — but not enmity toward others who are sincerely trying to live and find their way in life.

Oh, may we live our lives with more concern and kindliness for loved ones, more compassion for other people, more honesty, more gentleness in judgment, and even maybe more forgiving of ourselves, knowing that God lives, that life and loved ones are everlasting, that His law and power and purpose are over all — and thus find faith and peace, as we improve, repent, forgiving others, keeping His commandments, living the laws of health, the laws of happiness, indeed the laws of life — so living that, gently and sincerely, we can even forgive ourselves.

". . . while you are making other plans"

S omewhere we have read a sentence which says "Life is what happens to you while you are making other plans."[181] We are all subject to unforeseen events. We all need each other. No man ever knows when he will need another.

"There, but for the grace of God" am I,[182] is an oft-quoted phrase that applies to all people. A person in health, successful, happy, never knows when accident or illness or misfortune will reverse his situation. We all have reason to be grateful, to keep humble and to acknowledge the Source of all that is ours, and also to appreciate other people. And we all must face the reality that few things stay the same, except the basic laws and principles and purposes — the everlasting things of life, including the limitless possibilities of eternal progress.

But even when a change improves upon the past, it is sometimes difficult to adjust to. Growth is change. Learning is change. We never learn anything sincerely, and still think quite the same. Often we would like to stay where we are, be what we are, do what we are doing, keep things forever as they are, freeze life, in a sense — or so we suppose. But it isn't possible. Even if we did nothing to change, even if we resisted all modifying events, time and age would take over.

We have to prepare even for what we are unprepared for and do the best we can to protect ourselves, to insure ourselves, to keep our loved ones close, to keep our lives in health and happiness, to improve, to repent, to be grateful for all that is good — and to have faith and hope even on days that are down and discouraging.

And whatever happens in the interim, there is solid assurance that life is everlasting, and that eternal progress is its purpose, with justice and mercy, and with hope and faith more than equal to all our fears and frustrations. "Life is what happens while you are making other plans."

"Life is too short for mean anxieties."

—CHARLES KINGSLEY

PART 17

"There is nothing of which men are so fond, and . . . so care-less, as life."

—JEAN DE LA BRUYERE

"Who is man that he should forget . . . ?"

No matter how fast and far we may have moved, no matter how much we may have done or made, there are always unanswered questions, and always some searching: for purpose, for meaning, for assurance. And always there is need for the simple essentials: happiness, health, loved ones; duty, decency; service, sincerity.

And to all of these we ought to add humility — humility that comes with knowing how little we know of all there is to know. We discover a little, we control some things, sometimes. But nature, the weather, the seasons; age, illness; life and death, take us at times where they will, with all our little words and wisdom, in all the little parts we play, and with unceasing search, for truth and for ultimate answers.

Who knows how two cells join and divide — how some become an eye, some a tooth, some the hair of the head? Who can make a seed that will grow, or a blade of grass, a worm, or a single living cell?

Who can answer the questions God asked of Job so many centuries ago: "Where wast thou when I laid the foundations of the earth? When . . . all the sons of God shouted for joy? . . . declare, if thou hast understanding. . . . Where is the way where light dwelleth? . . . Who hath [caused] it to rain on the earth. . . ? Hast thou given the horse strength? . . . Doth the hawk fly by thy wisdom? Who hath put wisdom in the inward parts?"[183]

Who gave the body power to heal itself? Who gave instinct to animals? What would we do if Spring didn't come, if seeds didn't grow, if we didn't have our harvest?

Men have done much, learned much, but not enough to justify conceit and self-sufficiency. We still are children before an Infinite Father — with all our need for happiness, health, humility — loved ones — duty, decency; service, sincerity. And besides the classic question, "What is man, that thou art mindful of him,"[184] there is yet another: Who is man that he should forget?

. . . when a child begins to ask questions . . .

A person soon learns how little he knows when a child begins to ask questions. Children often penetrate us to the very center of our souls, and in their honest, searching innocence reveal to us our own dissembling.

They want to *know*. And we give them words. How do seeds grow? Why is it cold? What makes it dark? What makes my heart beat? What makes me move? Why? What? How do you know? Our first answers often don't satisfy

—and another "why" could follow every answer. Life is a search for all of us, as we face the fact that we know much less than we sometimes suppose.

What makes two cells join and divide and become a living person? How does memory work? Who gave the body wisdom to heal itself? Who gave animals their instincts? What makes water expand when it freezes? (If it didn't it would be a very different kind of world.) How was everything brought into being?

We discover, we observe. We use the forces of nature. We watch the operation of law. We explain with words — but without knowing much about the ultimate answers — the mind, the purpose, the prime mover, the origin of it all.

The veneer of sophistication and learning, is, after all, a comparatively shallow surface, and we are only using the facts and forces God has given. "I suspect," said one who is wise, "I suspect that men haven't discovered anything that the Creator was not already aware of,"[185] — and through it all there is ample evidence that the Maker and Administrator of all that is, is very much alive, and keeps Creation in its course, which is our assurance that spring will come, that the seasons will follow in succession, that we may have our harvest, and that life will go on according to plan and purpose, despite our troubles, large or little — and there is no place for the presumption or conceit of any person, however much he thinks he may have learned.

Humility, with faith and reverence and respect is becoming to us all. A person soon learns how little he knows when a child begins to ask questions.

Life . . . and questions that linger

Whether young or old, at whatever age, the question of life, of its length, of its everlastingness always lingers — sometimes insistently, sometimes suppressed. But the question becomes acute when someone close to us, someone cherished or admired or loved by us, leaves this life. And through the lingering thoughts, and sometimes shadowing doubts, and loneliness, and deep and yearning desire, comes the renewal of assurance that life *is* everlasting — for ourselves, and for our loved ones — and the evidence is overwhelming for the reality of eternal continuance.

"Let us accustom ourselves," wrote Maurice Maeterlinck, "to regard death as a form of life which we do not yet understand; . . . Death is but . . . a departure into an unknown filled with wonderful promises . . ."[186] And as to "our future beyond the grave, it is in no way necessary that we should have an answer to everything. . . . Total annihilation is impossible. . . . Neither a body nor a thought can drop out of the universe, out of time and space . . . for there is no place where anything ceases to be. . . . To be able to do away with a thing — that is to say, to fling it into nothingness — nothingness would have to exist; and, if it exists, under whatever form, it is no longer nothingness. . . ."[186]

There is no such thing as nothingness. "There is no such thing as immaterial matter."[187] As we continue, so do loved ones, so do principles, so do eternal purposes. And so, as we consider life, and death, and the reality of resurrection, we turn our thoughts to Him who showed the way of life and redeemed us from death. Oh may we use this moment of time, to live to realize the best of all there is of life with loved ones, through the endless opportunities of eternity.

Indifference to death . . . ?

Despite all differences of circumstances and situation, there is this that is common to us all: We all come alone into life and leave alone; and all who live for any long length see others come and go and have a sense of wonderment, and loss and loneliness.

Men have brooded about their own continuance as far back as the record reads: What is life? its purpose? What is our part in that purpose? Why do we love? Why do we lose those we love? Where are they? Shall we see them? And the crying of the human heart comes to all men, no matter how indifferent or secure they sometimes seem.

Men are not, cannot be, basically indifferent to death, even though they sometimes shut it from their minds. As Dr. Fosdick once wrote: "I am sure that some of you who think yourselves very modern, nonchalant about death and what lies after it, may some day run abruptly into an experience which will shake you to the depths. Somebody whom you love, the most priceless soul, it may be, you ever have loved, will die, and you will find that you cannot say that you are not interested, do not care, that it makes no difference to you what lies beyond death . . ."[188]

The God-given insight of prophets and poets, and all the inner awareness we have, assures us of eternal purpose, of our eternal ties and attachment to family and friends, and of the separate identity of ourselves, and of the pattern and the plan of a Divine Providence. And to those who wait and wonder, to those whose hearts are heavy, we would say with these words of Walter Owen, that these hoped for assurances, assuredly are so:

> When Time has done with me his worst and best,
>
> And my vault sealed, and mourners all gone home, . . .
>
> I shall not know when summer crowns the year,
>
> Though the brown bee creeps through the crannied stone, . . .
>
> Nor shall I heed when autumn's blazonry
> Hangs golden banners o'er my quiet head,
> Seasons and terms will be all one to me,
> I shall be less than earth. I shall be dead.

So men have said in their sad reckonings;
But men have reckoned wrong a world of
    things.[189]

"Blessed it is to know that neither distance nor death can truly separate those who love."[190]

And what of death . . . ?

Some of the loneliest of loneliness in life comes with loss of loved ones, and some of the most sobering concern comes with wondering where they are and when we again shall see them. Moved by such searching thoughts Andrew Jackson said: "Heaven will not be heaven to me if I do not meet my wife there."[191] Heaven to be heaven must have within it that which makes of heaven a wonderfully happy home — with loved ones as a part of all that makes completeness in an everlastingness of life.

How could it be otherwise? How could all this order, all this beauty — the earth, the sky, the sea, the glory of spring, the magnificent succession of all seasons, the love of life, the love of loved ones, the endless evidence of Providence, of plan, of purpose — the mind and memory of man — how could all this be other than eternal and of personal continuance.

"When I consider the wonderful activity of the mind," said Cicero, "so great a memory of what is past, and such capacity for penetrating the future; when I behold such a number of arts and sciences, and such a multitude of discoveries

. . . I believe and am firmly persuaded that a nature which contains so many things within itself cannot but be immortal."[192]

"Seems it strange that thou shouldst live forever," asked Edward Young. "Is it less strange that thou shouldst live at all?"[193] Life is the miracle, and that it should be always is no more a miracle than that it is at all. And so the meaning, the message of this moment: that He who gave us birth and life and loved ones has given us also the limitless possibilities of everlasting life.

And what of death?

Ay! it will come, — the bitter hour! — but bringing
A better love beyond, more subtle-sweet;
A higher road to tread, with happier singing,
And no cross-ways to part familiar feet![194]

Humble voyagers are we,
    Oe'r Life's dim, unsounded
    sea,
Seeking only some calm clime;—
    Touch us gently, gentle Time.

—BRYAN WALLER PROCTER

PART 18

"*I know this world is ruled by Infinite Intelligence. It required Infinite Intelligence to create it and it requires Infinite Intelligence to keep it on its course. . . . It is mathematical in its precision.*"

—THOMAS A. EDISON

Faith is not a theory

L ife is a search, with problems; disappointments often; an effort always, and with unanswered questions for us all — but with so much to make it worth all the effort: so much unknown to search, to learn; so much undone, so much to do, so much to be; so much of purpose — so apparent — of order, of meaning and of endless miracles — the miracle of spring's returning, the miracle of each day's dawning, the miracle of birth, of life, of loved ones — and so much reason for faith.

As the eminent physician, Sir William Osler said: "Nothing in life is more wonderful than faith."[195] Indeed, without it the world wouldn't run. "All the strength and force of man," said James F. Clark, "comes from his faith. . . ."[196] Faith is not a theory but a proved and practical force, and an absolute essential. Without it life wouldn't move forward.

All men have more faith than they sometimes suppose. Every time we plow and plant we show the faith we have — faith that summer will follow spring, faith that we shall have our harvest. Whenever we work, or learn, or invest, or plan for any future purpose, we show the faith we have.

Faith is the great moving force of repentance, of progress, of improvement. It is by faith that we build for the future. It is by faith that we can face the problems, the disappointments, the unanswered questions of life, a faith from out of which there comes a certainty of assurance that loved ones will be there, and waiting for us, in an everlastingness of life.

And in discouragement, with disappointments, with problems, we would well remember the miracle of life, the precious everlastingness of loved ones, and peace and purpose, as spring returns, and brings unnumbered reasons for our faith:

> For like a child, sent with a fluttering light
> To feel his way along a gusty night,
> Man walks the world. Again, and yet again,
> The lamp shall be by fits of passion slain;
> But shall not He who sent him from the door
> Relight the lamp once more, and yet once
> more?[197]

Chance could not have done it . . .

As men move farther out from the magnificent earth that God gave us, and look back on its awesome beauty, its movement, its precision and proportion, upon the wondrous working, and magnificent majesty of it all, we come with souls subdued to the quiet conviction of these simple words: "In the beginning God created the heaven and the earth. . . ."[198] Chance could not have done it. "And God saw every thing that he had made, and, behold, it was very good."[198]

Well, man, made in the image of God, has done much with his marvelous God-given mind, in the discovery and use of natural law. But much as man has done, he has scarcely touched the surface of all this majesty of meaning, and of infinite understanding.

Think a moment of the organizing and engineering and operation of it all — of keeping a world within a livable range of temperature; of air and water renewing themselves; of insect, animal and bacterial balance in infinite variety. And the creation is evidence of a Creator, design is evidence of the Designer, and law is evidence of its Maker and Administrator — evidence sufficient even for the most skeptical and unbelieving.

"When a load of bricks, dumped on a corner lot, can arrange themselves into a house;" wrote Bruce Barton, "when a handful of springs and screws and wheels, emptied onto a desk, can gather themselves into a watch, then and not until then will it seem sensible, to some of us at least, to believe that all . . . [this] could have been created . . . without any directing intelligence at all."[199] Then and only then will I believe that this was done by chance — or without eternal plan and purpose.

"Behind everything stands God. . . ." said Phillips Brooks. "Do not avoid, but seek, the great, deep, simple things of faith."[200] "And God saw every thing that he had made, and, behold, it was very good."

"more things than this world dreams of"

In some ways, it ought to be easier for this generation to have faith than any generation of the past — for many reasons — for one, that we have seen so many seeming miracles — miracles that man, by using nature's laws, has seen brought about.

Other generations didn't have so much evidence of the unseen sights and sounds, the unseen realities that are all around us. Other generations couldn't talk to distant loved ones with wires — or without wires. Other generations couldn't push a button and have the sights and sounds of all the earth immediately before them. Yet those sights and sounds were always there. Other generations didn't have the evidence of computers that could keep records of billions of people, in almost infinite detail.

When we see what man with his limited knowledge has been able to do in using some of the laws of nature, some of the laws of life, it should be much easier to understand how an Infinite Mind, an Infinite Administrator, the God of creation, could communicate with the prophets, could inspire the poets, could give promptings, warnings, guidance to people personally; could implant ideas and open the understanding of vast areas of truth to the sincere searcher. It should be easier for us to understand the possibilities of communication with the Infinite; the possibility, the power, the reality of prayer.

"More things are wrought by prayer than this world dreams of,"[201] as Tennyson said it. It should be easier for us to understand that an everlasting record is and can be kept. It should be easier for us to understand the limitless possibilities of life, by attuning ourselves to the Divine Source.

" . . . a man on his knees . . . "

"There is no limit to the reach of prayer"[202] — and not only is there no limit, but in many situations, no substitute — as many have come to know, among them Abraham Lincoln, from whom we cite some lines as to his dependence on Divine Providence, spoken at various times of need and acknowledgement:

"I went to my room and got down on my knees in prayer," he said. "Never before had I prayed with so much earnestness. . . . I felt that I must put all my trust in Almighty God. He gave our people the best country ever given to men. He alone could save it from destruction. . . . I prayed that He would not let the nation perish. . . . I felt that my prayer was answered. . . . I had no misgivings about the result. . . ."[203] "I have always taken counsel of Him, and have never adopted a course . . . without being assured, as far as I could be, of His approbation."[204] "I have been driven many times to my knees, by the overwhelming conviction that I had nowhere else to go. My own wisdom and that of all about me seemed insufficient for that day."[205] "I not only believe that Providence is not unmindful of the struggle . . . [but] that if we do not do right God will let us go our way to our ruin; and that if we do right, He will lead us safely out of this wilderness . . ."[206] "The ways of God are mysterious and profound beyond comprehension . . . there is nothing left but for the heart of man to take up faith and believe and trust where it cannot reason."[207] "We cannot but believe that He who made the world still governs it."[208] ". . . I now leave, not knowing when or whether ever I may return, with a task before me greater than that which rested upon Washington. Without the assistance of that Divine Being, who ever attended him, I cannot succeed. With that assistance I cannot fail. Trusting in Him who can go with me, and remain with you, and be everywhere for good, let us confidently hope that all will yet be well. To His care commending you, as I hope in your prayers you will commend me, I bid you an affectionate farewell."[209] Thus spoke Abraham Lincoln, as he poured out his heart to the God and Father of us all, in earnest need and acknowledgment.

. . . for directions on how to live life . . .

Where should we — or can we go — for directions on how to live life? Perhaps we can draw a parallel. Where would we go for directions on how to use a machine, a car, or a complex piece of equipment? Who knows most about what things are made for, how they should be used and cared for, what they are designed to do? Obviously, the designer or maker of a machine would be the one most likely to prepare a manual of instructions pertaining to it.

And so likewise, in life, the Creator would know most about its purposes, about people, about their possibilities. The Maker would know why moderation, morality, labor, respect for law are essential for peace and health and happiness.

He has given us a marvellous mind, marvellous physical faculties, and has counselled us to do some things and not to do others. He has counselled us not to clutter our lives or consciences with unwholesome habits, or careless living, or unbecoming conduct. It is natural that it should be so. One cannot conceive of a parent's not being interested in everything that pertains to his children: their physical, mental, moral and spiritual health, and happiness. And one cannot conceive of the Father of us all not being interested in everything that pertains to His children. And so He has given us standards, counsel, requirements, commandments, laws, rules of life to realize our highest possibilities, our highest happiness. Where else would we turn? Whom else could we trust with our everlasting lives? There are many brilliant men on earth but none who knows enough.

To those distressed, to those with problems, to those who are searching for answers that satisfy: look beyond the superficial, beyond the surface, beyond the shifting theories, the irresponsible permissiveness, the false assumptions. Look to

the meaning and purpose and peace of life, and
its limitless, everlasting possibilities. Turn to
the Maker and Administrator of all things for
the directions you so much seek.

*"I felt so young, so strong, so
sure of God."*

—Elizabeth Barrett Browning

PART 19

"O God! Put back Thy universe and give me yesterday."

—HENRY ARTHUR JONES

If we don't change
direction . . .

There is a simple axiom which says: "A straight line is the shortest distance between two points." And added to this we offer this simple assertion: If we don't change direction, we will arrive at where we are going. This applies to people personally, to companies, to communities, to countries. If we don't change direction, we will arrive at where we are going.

If, for example, we are running more deeply in debt, we shall continue to run deeper into debt — unless we change direction. If we are doing anything detrimental to health and happiness, if we don't change direction we shall arrive at ill health and unhappiness.

If our relationships with our loved ones are deteriorating, if we are moving toward less happiness in marriage, less happiness at home, sincerely we should search ourselves, and see what part we are playing in the downhill process, before we bring heartbreak to ourselves and to the lives of our loved ones.

If we are falsifying, if we are engaging in small degrees of dishonesty, taking things that belong to others and not to us, breaking the law, not being quite truthful or forthright, not giving quite an honest day of effort — if persistently we are moving in such directions, we shall arrive at where they take us.

If we are not taking the trouble to learn, to study, to apply ourselves, we shall arrive at wherever we're going, knowing less than we ought to know.

Sometimes we live with the hope that something will happen to take us in a different direction. And it may be that something outside ourselves might do so. But even if someone else were to provide us with every opportunity, there would still have to be within us the will, the willingness to learn, to repent, to improve.

The way to change is to change. The way to repent is to depart from former practices — to change direction, to turn to the right road. If we don't change direction, we will arrive at where we are going.

"When people once are in the wrong . . ."

"A man who has committed a mistake and doesn't correct it," said Confucius, "is committing another mistake."[210] Having in mind that all of us make mistakes, we turn to some further citations:

"Some often repent, yet never reform;" said Bonnell Thornton, "they resemble a man travelling in a dangerous path, who frequently starts and stops, but never turns back."[211]

"Repentance may begin instantly," observed Henry Ward Beecher, "but reformation often requires a sphere of years."[212]

And from Samuel Johnson: "As long as one lives he will have need of repentance."[120]

Now back to the beginning: "A man who has committed a mistake and doesn't correct it, is committing another mistake." There is no virtue in postponing repentance to some particular time. There *is* virtue in repenting in the present — in doing so this very day. It isn't ever altogether easy — and it comes down, finally, to a question of character — wanting to, willingness, working at it.

If there are mistakes, they can be acknowledged. If there are habits we shouldn't have, they can begin to be conquered. If, because of us, there are hurt hearts and offended feelings, it is for us to make amends.

Others can encourage. Others can help. But no one else can repent for us. The obligation and the opportunity are ours — and what *we* do will determine the difference. And if we don't repent, if we don't change direction, we will arrive at whatever end our present attitudes and actions tend to take us. "He who chooses the beginning of a road, chooses the place to which it leads."[25]

> When people once are in the wrong
> Each line they add is much too long;
> Who fastest walks, but walks astray,
> Is only furthest from his way.[213]

"A man who has committed a mistake and doesn't correct it, is committing another mistake."

"If something needs doing . . ."

" If something needs doing, do it; the more plainly, directly, honestly, the better."[214] These words of David Starr Jordan suggest two facets of an insistent subject, namely, the remorse that comes from doing what we shouldn't do, and the frustration that comes from not doing what we should do.

To look a moment at the latter: There are many reasons for not moving forward effectively: timidity, indolence, indecision, lack of encouragement, fear of failure. But foremost among them would seem to be indecision. And so the years go by, with many wishing to do differently, to develop, to lift their lives; but habits, obligations, indifference, or sometimes simply not knowing how, keep many from trying, from getting going.

We all waste time in indecision. We all waste opportunities. And if we were to put a meter on ourselves, we would find we waste much time in brooding, drifting, wishing, worrying.

Too often we seem resigned to settling for what we are rather than for what we could become. And yet, all process, all improvement in any process have come because someone assumed that something could be better done, and was willing to try to do it — often humble, unpretentious people who simply used a little common sense.

On the personal side, we often excuse ourselves for delaying what we know we ought to do — delaying learning, teaching, taking time for our children; delaying the settling of quarrels, clearing up misunderstandings with our loved ones, being a little kinder; delaying breaking bad habits, meeting obligations, repenting, keeping the commandments, and finding personal peace.

"Men should do many things of their own free will"[215] — and life can take on new and solid satisfaction if we commit ourselves to facing facts, to doing what should be done. "If something needs doing, do it; the more plainly, directly, honestly, the better."

The beauty of good beginnings

"There is a human instinct," said Phillips Brooks, "which tells us that our life, while it is meant to have a great continuousness . . . is no less meant to be full of new starts. . . . It is the same life from its beginning to its end, . . . yet forever is . . . refreshing its forces. . . . It loves to turn sharp corners into unseen ways [and] start out with the new birth of a new resolution. . . . In many ways there is a sense of stir and start about us. . . . It is wonderful how ingenious men will be in making artificial new starts in their lives, . . . It is sad indeed when any man comes to that state in which each new day does not seem in some true sense to begin the world anew, recalling every departed hope and brightening every faded color of the night before. . . . He must be dull who does not feel . . . the beauty of beginnings . . . the newness of each new day, . . . [which] keeps [us] from degenerating into [monotony and] mechanical routine . . ."[216]

"Look over the world," said Carlyle, "Is it not wonderful, . . . if your eyes were open! This Earth, God made it for you; appointed paths in it; you can live in it; go to and fro on it."[217] "O my young friends, the world is beautiful and . . . life is full of promise."[216]

Each new day is a blessing; each hour is an opportunity. Work at it, learn from it, enjoy it, improve it, repent, improve yourselves, respect and live by law and by God-given, time-proved principles.

Thank God that there is purpose, that there is plan, that there is order and design and wisdom over-all and that we have another day, another hour, another chance, another season to shape ourselves.

Before us all there is always the new beginning, and also the endlessness of everlasting life . . . "that never need be stale to any of us."[216] Thank God for the beauty of good beginnings — and that there is no one who cannot improve upon the past.

The past is to learn from
... not to live in ...

From a thoughtful mood, for a thoughtful moment comes this reminder: The past is to learn from, not to live in. Our thoughts move in many directions, with the events of each day, with the mood of each moment. We waver often between discouragment and confidence, between regret and gratitude, wishing we *had* done better and hoping we *might* do better — searching ourselves, looking for values, for guidelines in life — loving the earth we live on, yet somehow sensing that we are on a journey that moves us on, through time and to eternity.

We all have days of discouragement. "Sometimes the hardest thing in life is simply to put one foot in front of the other — to keep going," as one observer said, "And, sometimes, the most worthwhile things . . . are accomplished . . . by people who are struggling not for greatness, . . . but simply . . . to keep going."[218] And there is quiet heroism and goodness and earnest purpose on the part of many wonderful people, despite all failures and imperfections.

There is evil in the world. There is also good. It is for us to learn and choose between the two; to increase in self-discipline, in competence, in kindness; to keep going — putting one foot in front of the other — one day, one hour, one moment, one task at a time. There is no point in giving up in regret, for life is a process — a process of repentance, of improvement, and will justify all the trial and error and effort, as we keep moving, with patience and purpose.

"Have courage for the *great* sorrows of life, and patience for the *small* ones;" wrote Victor Hugo, "and when you have laboriously accomplished your daily task, go to sleep in peace. God is awake."[219]

The past is to learn from, not to live in.

"No one can ask honestly or hope fully to be delivered from temptation unless he has himself honestly and firmly determined to do the best he can to keep out of it."

—JOHN RUSKIN

PART 20

> "Let us be patient, tender, wise,
> forgiving, In this strange task of
> living . . ."
>
> —MARTIN ARMSTRONG

"All your danger is in discord . . ."

There are these lines from Longfellow:

> All your strength is in your union.
> All your danger is in discord.
> Therefore be at peace henceforward,
> And as brothers live together.[220]

And he might have added — as husbands and wives live together, parents, children, as business partners; as neighbors and nations live together. "All your strength is in your union. All your danger is in discord . . ."

The strength, the joy of life is in harmony at home, at work, in the world — and the danger of discord could hardly be over-emphasized. Discord is among the greatest tools of the Devil — quarreling, contention, friction in families, husbands, wives, parents, children, neighbors, nations quarreling and contending with each other, almost as if without awareness that a little friction can go a long way — and to cite a recent source, "can trigger chain reactions," and "shake the whole delicate balance of office or workshop or home [or of the whole world] . . . Friction does not have to be screechy, . . . to be dangerous and evil."[221]

Small frictions grow to large ones, and lead to hostility, and happiness leaves the home, the heart, and the hope and joy of life are less. More and more we need to know that families, neighbors, men and nations can destroy each other in quarreling and controversy. More and more we need to "turn the heart of the fathers to the children, and the heart of the children to their fathers . . ."[222]

A sense of belonging, a secure place in the family circle, is forever among life's most priceless possessions. ". . . if ye are not one ye are not mine,"[223] said our Savior.

God grant that husbands, wives, children, parents, partners, fellow workers, men of all faiths, indeed that all the children of God may turn hearts toward each other — and also that a man should not quarrel with himself inside, but keep the commandments and have a quiet conscience. "All your strength is in your union. All your danger is in discord . . ."

"We don't stumble over mountains"

Somewhere we have heard this old, yet interesting observation: "We don't stumble over mountains." It seems we stumble over small things mostly. It is by small steps and seemingly inconsequential decisions that we arrive at where we are. If we were to know the inside of wasted lives, of failures, unhappy families, we would likely find that small things loom very large.

Serious problems seem to begin with small things, and often at early ages. Homes, families, marriages are broken often by little things, annoyances, small acts of thoughtlessness, lack of courtesy and consideration, lack of honesty in little things — small falsehoods, small deceptions in accounting for time or money. The breaking point may add up to something major and dramatic, but leading to it are small steps: inconsideration, irritations, indiscretions.

Sometimes people protest their love and loyalty and offer to do almost *anything* to make amends, but leave the little things undone. There are those who profess they would lay down their lives, but who won't serve or sacrifice in the small day-to-day duties and discipline. Some have the all or nothing attitude. But life isn't like that. Those who insist on all or nothing are likely to have little or less.

The years are made of minutes. Much of life is made of memories, warm and happy memories of small kindnesses and consideration, of courtesy, of constancy, consistency; a mother's attentive care, a father's kindliness, a child's thankfulness; thoughtfulness each day, not grand and rare and obvious outward acts — not all at once, but small and constant ways as each occasion comes.

If we want happiness with loved ones, and peace, and quiet conscience, we need to learn the little lessons, the small services, the continuing kindnesses, the habitual acts of honesty, the constancy of cleanliness — not just one big washing.

"We don't stumble over mountains." We stumble over small things mostly.

On living with imperfect people - including ourselves

One of the urgent lessons of life is to learn how to live with imperfect people — not only with the imperfections of others but also with imperfections we see in ourselves. It is often true that we do not even please ourselves, or at least not consistently, completely so. And if we do not altogether please ourselves, it should be easy for us to understand why often we are not altogether pleased with others.

Life is variable for all of us. Sometimes we are sad, fearful, discouraged, sometimes even when we have no apparent reason to be. Our troubles trouble us less at some times than they do at others; not necessarily that the troubles are less, but we are able to live with our troubles at some times better than others.

Human problems are complex. There are battles within ourselves, and battles outside ourselves. The good strives with us, the spirit that would lead to truth and peace and self-respect — the spirit that pleads to be heard and heeded — and finds itself in competition with the spirit that would tempt us to compromise, to be critical, indifferent, rebellious, to relax our standards, and do what sometime we shall surely regret.

And since everyone has his struggles, his better days and worse ones, his good impulses and less worthy ones, his arguments inside himself; since all of us need understanding, forgiveness, encouragement, all of us would well give compassionate consideration to others. One quality of character most needed in this world is compassion for other people. One of the urgent lessons of life is to learn how to live with imperfect people — including ourselves. And if we are not altogether pleased with us, it should be easy to understand why we are not altogether pleased with others. "Every man," said Henry Ward Beecher, "should have a good-sized cemetery in which to bury the faults of his friends."[212]

" ... what to overlook"
- and when

"The art of being wise," said William James, "is the art of knowing what to overlook."[224]

Life without friends, without loved ones would be too altogether empty. But since people are not perfect, our companionship with people is never perfect. When we associate with people we take them with their imperfections. But over-emphasizing imperfections leads to unpleasantness, unhappiness, disillusionment. This is so in marriage, in the home, the family, among friends, in every relationship in life.

One of the greatest lessons of life is learning to help people to improve without making them resentful, or shattering their confidence, or destroying our influence with them. Correcting people when others are present is especially embarrassing, and correcting with sarcasm is always hurtful in effect.

We ourselves never do all we ought to do as well as we ought to do it. No one of us is possesessed of all virtues, or abilities, or flawless performance. There is no one who is *never* forgetful. No one can always follow a schedule, always have meals precisely on time (or always be there precisely on time), or always have the house look as if company were expected, or always have everything precisely in place.

Man is not merely a machine — he is much more — but even machines need understanding, and even machines make errors. There is much to be overlooked in all of us — and some things that should *not* be overlooked. But even these can be dealt with in tact and helpfulness, choosing the time, the place, the mood, the method. There are ways of suggesting, of holding back, of timing, of correcting in kindness, instead of harsh, cruel, blundering correction that makes people feel small, hurt, resentful.

There are times to correct and times not to. There are ways to correct and ways not to. "The art of being wise is the art of knowing *what* to overlook" — and *when*.

. . . the miserable misunderstandings . . .

Sometimes in our thoughtless rushing about we become impersonal and preoccupied with *things* that matter less, and overlook the hearts and feelings and inmost needs of *people* who matter more.

In the sometimes rough abrasiveness of crowded days and things to do, we well would pause and think upon our lives and loved ones, upon the needs, the problems, the preciousness and importance to us of people personally, and do some searching of ourselves.

For such a time Phillips Brooks has left some lines that may turn hearts and lives to loved ones, and bring friends and families closer, and more of peace inside ourselves: "You who are letting miserable misunderstandings run on from year to year, meaning to clear them up some day;" he said, "You who are keeping wretched quarrels alive because you cannot quite make up your mind that now is the day to sacrifice your pride and [settle] them: You who are passing men sullenly upon the street, not speaking to them out of some silly spite; You who are letting . . . [someone's] heart ache for a word of appreciation or sympathy, which you mean to give him someday; If you only could know and see and feel, all of a sudden, *the time is short*, how it would break the spell! How you would go instantly and do the thing which you might never have another chance to do."[6]

If only we could see how swiftly life goes — how few are the hours — how much less likely we would be to pamper pride, to fail to take first steps to right old wrongs, to fail to shorten distances between us and others; how less likely we would be to live aloof when hearts are crying to be understood, aching to remove misunderstanding. And how much more honest and at ease we would be, with less pretense, less sparring for position, more willingness to make amends.

We come alone. We leave alone. We are not here long. Oh, if, please God, we could somehow strip away the impersonal aloofness, the indifferent and sometimes cruel facade, clear up the wretched quarrels and misunderstandings, bring loved ones closer, and become our better selves.

"The world is too narrow for two fools a quarrelling."

—THOMAS FULLER

Epilogue

Not Understood

"Not understood. We move along asunder,
   Our paths grow wider as the seasons creep
Along the years; we marvel and we wonder
   Why life is life, and then we fall asleep,
         Not understood.

"Not understood. We gather false impressions
   And hug them closer as the years go by,
Til virtues often seem to us transgressions;
   And thus men rise and fall and live and die,
         Not understood.

"Not understood. Poor souls with stunted vision
   Oft measure giants by their narrow gauge.
The poisoned shafts of falsehood and derision
   Are oft impelled 'gainst those who mould the
      age,
         Not understood.

"Not understood. The secret springs of action,
   Which lie beneath the surface and the show,
Are disregarded; with self-satisfaction
   We judge our neighbors as they often go,
         Not understood.

"Not understood. How trifles often change us.
   The thoughtless sentence or the fancied slight
Destroys long years of friendships, and estranges
      us,
   And on our souls there falls a freezing blight:
         Not understood.

"Not understood. How many breasts are aching,
   For lack of sympathy? Ah! day to day,
How many cheerless, lonely hearts are breaking!

How many noble spirits pass away,
      Not understood.

"O God, that men would see a little clearer,
    Or judge less harshly where they cannot see!
O God, that men would draw a little nearer
    To one another! They'd be nearer Thee
      And understood."[225]

—THOMAS BRACKEN

Index of Subjects

Abstinence, 114, 115
Accidents, 114, 118, 168
Age, old, 18, 19, 53-60
Alone living, 23, 24, 118, 177
Anger, 107, 108
Appearances, 128, 129 (see also Clean)
Appetites, 113, 164 (see also Impairment of mind and body)
Attitude(s), 14, 15, 23, 27, 77

Balance in life 54, 55, 75, 80, 159 (see also Moderation)
Begin(nings), 86, 89, 113, 197, 198
Blessings, 147 (see also Thanksgiving)
Body abuse of (see Impairment of mind and body)
Bored, 15, 16 (see also Indifference)
Brothers, as, live together, 203

Calm, inner, 107, 108, 167
Career, 63-70 (see also Education)
Cause (see Consequences)
Chance, 168, 184, 185, 198
Change, 133, 168
Character, 69, 101, 103, 104, 110, 116, 117, 126, 127, 130, 133, 155, 157, 195 (see also Honesty)
Chastity 125, 134, 136, 137 (see also Virtue)
Children, 34-39, 63, 78, 96, 97, 116, 117, 129, 159, 160, 174 (see also Family, Home, Parents)
Choice, 13, 17, 18, 84, 88, 129, 145, 157, 199 (see also Decisions)
Christ (see God)
Christmas, 159, 160
Clean(liness), 14, 15, 19, 46, 96, 121, 124, 125, 128, 129, 136, 137, 149, 205 (see also Impairment of mind and body)

Commandments (see God, commandments of)
Commencement, 63 - 70 (see also Children, Parents)
Communication, 36 (see also Children, Parents)
Compassion, 106, 107, 167, 206, 207
Compensation, 94, 109, 147 (see also Consequences)
Competence, 17, 65, 68, 69, 86, 199 (see also Education)
Compromise, 29, 137, 206
Conduct, 99 (see also Consequences)
Confidence, 67, 199, 207
Conscience, 14, 65, 76, 91-100, 103, 106, 145, 164, 204 205 (see also Peace, inner)
Consequences, 94, 99, 110, 134, 145 (see also Compensation)
Consistency, 116, 205 (see also Endure)
Contentment, 74, 75, 87
Conventions of society, 144
Counsel, 15, 26, 36, 37, 144 (see also God, counsel of)
Country, character of our, 149, 150 (see also Earth)
Courage, 103, 104
Courtesy, 37, 116, 117, 205
Crowd, 30 (see also Popularity)

Death, 118, 154, 155, 158, 176-178 (see also Immortality, Life everlasting)
Debt, 71-74, 78, 89, 193 (see also Money)
Decisions, 13, 67, 79, 205 (see also Choice)
Delay, 195, 197
Direction(s), 188 - 190, 193, 194
Disappointment, 81-90, 106, 185 (see also Discouragement)

[215]

[217]

Survival, 149 (see also Lawless, Safety)

Talent, 103, 104, 116
Teach(ing), 63-70, 123, 129, 137 (see also Prepare)
Temper, 107, 108
Temperance, 114, 115, 148 (see also Balance)
Tempt(ation), 28, 86, 106, 135, 200, 206
Tested, looked good until, 134, 135
Thanksgiving, 157, 158
Thoughts, 119, 123, 124, 163
Thrill of a moment, 85
Time, waste of, 53, 54, 86, 161-170, 196, 209
Tolerance, 148 (see also Endure)
Trifles, 44, 45, 164, 165, 204, 205 (see also Little Things)
Trouble, 206 (see also Discouragement, Problems)
Trust(worthy), 79, 134 (see Integrity)

Uncertainty, 136 (see also Future)
Unessentials (see Little Things, Trifles)
Unhappines, 98, 99 (see also Happiness)
Understanding, 167, 206, 209, 213, 214 (see also Misunderstanding)

Virtue, 94, 104, 124 (see also Chastity, Impairment of mind and body)

Work, 13, 54-60, 69, 77, 78, 87, 104 (see also Prepare)
Worry, 89 (see also Problems)
World (see Earth, wonders of)

Youth, 15, 23-27, 55, 63-70, 116, 125, 138 (see also Children, Clean, Counsel, Impairment of mind and body, Parents, Prepare, Restlessness)

Index of Quotations

1. Ralph Waldo Emerson, 13, 70
2. Ibid., *Compensation,* 14
3. Dr. Neal A. Maxwell, 14
4. Attributed to Abraham Lincoln, 15, 98
5. Shakespeare, *Hamlet,* Act i, sc. 5, 15
6. Phillips Brooks (1835-93), Am. Epis. bishop, 17, 209
7. Robert Frost, *The Road Not Taken,* 18
8. Rotary Club Bulletin of Graham, Texas. Author unknown, 18
9. William James, Hibbert Lectures at Oxford, 18
10. Book of Mormon, Alma 41:10, 19, 137
11. Lawrence A. Appley, *Managers in Action,* 24
12. Benjamin Franklin, *Autobiography,* 26
13. Hendrick Van Loon, *Geography,* 29
14. Samuel Goldwyn, "Why Everything Counts: You always meet people a second time," *This Week Magazine,* January 21, 1962, 29
15. Edward Fitzgerald, *Polonius,* 30
16. Henry Wadsworth Longfellow, *Maidenhood,* 33
17. Doctrine and Covenants, 121:43, 35
18. Strickland Gillilan *The Reading Mother,* 35

19. Hannie Struve, *Sunrise Magazine,* July 1967, 36
20. Robert M. Neal, "I get to KNOW my boy," *Parents' Magazine,* February 1946, 36
21. Gary Cleveland Myers, *A Parent's Prayer,* 37
22. *Time* Essay: "On Being an American Parent," December 15, 1967, 37
23. Phillips Brooks, *T h e Mother's Wonder,* 37
24. Ibid., *The Beautiful Gate of the Temple,* 38
25. Author unknown, 38, 78, 89, 128
26. Harold B. Lee, 38
27. Shakespeare, *Hamlet,* Act i, 40
28. Dr. William Lyon Phelps, quoting an unknown writer, 44
29. Ibid., *"Marriage Is What You Make It," Delineator* August 1932, 43
30. Temple Bailey, "T h e Bride Who Makes Her Dreams C o m e True," *Ladies Home Journal,* June 1912, 44
31. Dr. Paul Popenoe, "Make Your Marriage a Partnership," *L a d i e s' Home Journal,* J u n e 1942, 44
32. D. Willson, "Recipes for Happy Marriage," *Good Housekeeping,* June 1933, 45
33. Magaret W. Jackson, "Marriage as it Ought To Be," *Ibid.,* J u n e 1933, 45
34. David O. McKay, General Conference Address, October 3, 1969, 45
35. Dr. Paul Popenoe, *Ladies Home Journal,* February 1942, p. 22, 46
36. Cornelius Cabot, "How Shall a Young Man Decide?" *Ibid.,* M a r c h 1914, p. 17, 46

37. Corinne Low, "Which? The Bride: A Liability or an Asset?" *Delineator,* June 1919, 47
38. David O. McKay, Conference Address, April 4, 1969, 47
39. Hubert S. Howe, M.D., "Can't I Save My Marriage?", in an article by Sarah Comstock *Good Housekeeping,* January 1935, 48
40. Dorothy Walworth, "Don't Be Afraid to Say Y o u ' r e Sorry," Ibid., April 1942, 50
50. Jack London (Citation from the Jack London State Historic Park folder), 53
51. William Lyon Phelps, 54, 59
52. Lucius Annaeus Seneca 4 B.C.-65 A.D.), Rom. stoic philos., 54
53. Samuel Johnson, *T h e Idler,* No. 72, 54
54. Old Testament, Genesis 3:17, 55
55. Thomas Carlyle, *Inaugural* Address, Edinburgh, 1866, 55
56. Sir William Osler, 56
57. Phillips B r o o k s, *The Light of the World and Other Sermons: Identity and Variety,* 57
58. Cicero, *On Old Age,* 57
59. George B. E m e r s o n (1797-1881), Am. educ., 58
60. Anna R. Lindsay, *What Is Worth While?* 58
61. Dolores De Rio, in an interview with Joe Hyams, published in *This Week* magazine, January 12, 1964, 58
62. Rev. Ralph W. Sockman, *Age Has Its Advantages,* 58
63. William Cowper, *Retirement Poems,* 1782, 58

64. "The Country Parson," *Evening Tribune,* S a n Diego, California, 58

65. Kenneth S. Beam, 59

66. H. A. H o l l e , M. D., American Medical Association, 59

67. Karle Wilson B a k e r , *D e s k Drawer Anthology: P o e m s for the American People,* 60

68. Samuel Johnson, *Rasselas,* ch. 41, 64

69. John Sloan D i c k e y , President of Dartmouth College, as quoted by The Rt. Rev. John E. Hines in a Newcomen Address, Jan. 25, 1968, 65

70. Henry Adams, The Edu c a t i o n of H e n r y Adams, ch. 20, 65

71. G e o r g e Eliot, *Scenes from C l e r i c a l Life: Amos Barton,* 65

72. Benjamin Disraeli, 66

73. Marcus Aurelius, *Meditations,* Bk. xii, sec. 17, 68

74. New Testament, Luke 14:28-30, 74

75. *Carnegie Quarterly* bulletin, Vol. xvii, No. 3, 74

76. Daniel D e F o e (1661-1731), Eng. auth., 75, 107

77. Samuel Smiles, *Character: Duty — Truthfulness,* ch. vii, 77

78. Old Testament, Genesis 1:28, 77

79. Gamaliel B r a d f o r d, "Journal," 1916, cited in *H a r p e r ' s Monthly,* March 1933, p. 419, 83

80. John Milton, 84

81. Alexander Pope, *T h e Universal Prayer,* 84

82. John Erskine, cited in *On the Meaning of Life,* p. 41, by Durant, 84

83. New Testament, Matthew 5:45, 84

84. George M a c D o n a l d (1824-1905), Scot. novelist, 84

85. Sir John Lubbock, first Baron Avebury, 85

86. T h o m a s DeWitt Talmage (1832-1902), Am. clergy, 86

87. Harry Emerson Fosdick, *On Being a Real Person: Mastering Depression,* 86

88. Robert Louis Stevenson, 87

89. Ian Maclaren, as quoted in Arthur John Gossip, *From the Edge of the Crowd,* 87

90. Herbert G. Wells (1866-1946), Eng. novelist and hist., 87

91. Book of Mormon, II Nephi 2:11, 88

92. Comment accredited to t h e motion p i c t u r e *Shenandoah,* 88

93. B e n j a m i n Disraeli, *Sybil,* Bk. i, ch. 8, 88

94. Matthew Arnold, *The Scholarly Gypsy,* St. 21, 88

95. Plato, 90

96. Madam de Stael (1766-1817), Fr. authoress, 93

97. Francis Bowen (1811-90), Am. philos., 93

98. George Crabbe, *Tales:* No. xiv, *The Struggles of Conscience,* 93

99. Leszinski S t a n i s l a u s, (1677-1766), King of Poland, 93

100. Elbert Hubbard, *Philistine,* Vol. xi, p. 77, 95

101. Emerson, *Education,* 96

102. New Testament, Matthew 18:6, 96

103. William Ellery C h a n ning, *On the Elevation of the Laboring Classes,* 96

104. Doctrine and Covenants 93:40, 97

105. M a r k Twain, *Huckle-berry Finn*: *You Can't Pray a Lie,* ch. 31, 100

106. Samuel Smiles, *Charac-ter*: *Courage,* ch. 5, 103

107. Phillips Brooks, *Twenty Sermons*: *Sermon* xviii, 104

108. Red Barber, *Walk in the Spirit*: *Mr. Rickey,* 104

109. J o s e p h L. Townsend, *Let Us Oft Speak Kind Words,* 105

110. Henry Wadsworth Long-fellow, 106

111. Thomas C. Haliburton (1696-1865), Nova Sco-tian humorist, 107

112. Old Testament, Genesis 4:5, 108

113. Seneca, *On Anger,* 108

114. Brigham Young, J. D. 11:255, 108

115. Louis Leon de Saint Just (1767 - 94), Fr. leader, 108

116. George Herbert (1593-1633), Eng. divine and poet, 108

117. William George Jordan, *The Majesty of Calm-ness,* 109

118. Editorial, "Meeting Life Squarely," *The Outlook,* Dec. 20, 1916, 109

119. Shakespeare, *H e n r y VIII,* 110

120. Samuel Johnson (1709-84), Eng. auth. and lexi-cographer, 113, 195

121. John L o c k e , *S o m e Thoughts Concerning Education,* 113

122. Thomas a Kempis, *The Imitation of Christ,* 113

123. G e o r g e B. Cheever (1807 - 90), Am. clergy, 114

124. Samuel Johnson, *More Johnsoniana,* N o . 467, 114

125. Frederick K. S t a m m , ''C o u r t e s y ,'' *Good Housekeeping,* January 1937, 116

126. Samuel Smiles, *Charac-ter*: *Home Power,* ch. 2, 117

127. Ibid., *Influence of Char-acter,* ch. 1, 117

128. John Muir, *My First Summer in the Sierra,* 117

129. John Donne, in the 17th century *Meditation,* 118

130. Louisa May Alcott, 123

131. See Old Testament, Pro-verbs 23:7, 123

132. William A. Orton, *Post-Script,* September 1968, 123

133. Dr. Frank Crane, *Four Minute Essays*: *Slov-enly Thought,* 124

134. Doctrine and Covenants 121:45, 124

135. David O. McKay, *In-structor,* August 1966, 125

136. New Testament, Gala-tians 5:16, 22, 125

137. *Hugh B. Brown,* You *and Your Marriage,* p. 66, 125

138. New Testament, II Cor-inthians 6:17, 18, 125

139. The First Presidency, April 6, 1942, 125

140. Emerson, *Letters a n d Social Aims*: *S o c i a l Aims,* 126

141. Cicero *De Officiis,* Bk. i, ch. 19, 126

142. New T e s t a m e n t , I Thess. 5:22, 128

143. Gilbert K. Chesterton, 133

144. Alexander Pope, *Essays on Criticism,* 133

145. New Testament, I Cor. 14:40, 134

146. Joe E. Whitesides, *Re-pair Through Resolu-tion,* 134

147. The R o y a l Bank of Canada Monthly Letter, Vol. 50, No. 2, 138

148. Phillips B r o o k s , *The Light of the World and*

O t h e r   Sermons: The Choice Young Man, 138

149. Old Testament, Exodus 19:3, 5, 8, 16; 20:1-22, 140

150. Lida A. C h u r c h i l l, "Freedom that Is Bondage," *Delineator,* January 1907, 145

151. Francois La Rochefoucauld (1630-80), Fr. moralist, 145

152. Doctrine and Covenants 130:20, 145

153. M-Men - Gleaners MIA youth o r g a n i z a t i o n, 1929, The Church of Jesus Christ of Latter-day Saints, 146

154. Dr. Frank Crane, *Four Minute Essays: P a y, Pay, Pay!* 147

155. John Philpot C u r r a n (1750-1817), Irish Judge and Orator, quoted by Maj. - Gen. J. G. Harbord, 148

156. M a j o r General J. G. Harboard, *The Relative Position of the Individual Under Democratic and Totalitarian States,* delivered at University of Virginia, 148

157. Joseph Smith, *The Principles of Religion,* 148

158. Doctrine and Covenants 101:80, 148

159. Dean Russell, pamphlet on *The Bill of Rights.* 148

160. Doctrine and Covenants 101:77, 78, 149

161. Charles Sumner, Oration on the True Grandeur of Nations, delivered in Boston, July 4, 1845, 149

162. The Scout Oath a n d Motto, 149

163. Abraham Lincoln, Address b e f o r e Y o u n g Men's L y c e u m, of Springfield, Illinois, Jan. 27, 1838, 150

164. Accredited to Dwight D. Eisenhower, 150

165. Abraham Lincoln, Annual Message to Congress, 1862, 150

166. Dr. Arthur H. Compton (1928 Nobel Prize winner in Physics), 155

167. David Macbeth M o i r, *Casa Wappy,* 155

168. See "A Man and his Father," by Carl Van Doren, *Good Housekeeping,* December 1948, 156

169. N e w Testament, John 5:19, 157

170. Ibid., Matthew 5:48, 157

171. To Charles W. Eliot, by Samuel A. Eliot, *What I Owe to My Father,* 157

172. Shakespeare, *II Henry VI,* Act ii, sc. 1, 158, 159

173. William P e n n, *Some Fruits of Solitude,* 159

174. Henry Wadsworth Longfellow, *I Heard the Bells on Christmas Day,* 160

175. Edward Young, *Night Thoughts,* 163

176. Longfellow, *Hyperion,* Bk. ii, ch. 6, 163

177. Benjamin Franklin, *The Way to Wealth,* 164

178. Emerson, Self-Reliance, 164

179. Diogenes (412-323 B.C.), Gr. philos., 165

180. Arthur Brisbane, as reprinted in *Sunshine Magazine,* 165

181. A. J. Marshall, 168

182. John Bradford, *Works,* Vol. II (Also credited to others, including Richard Baxter, John Bunyan, John Wesley), 168

183. Old Testament, Job, ch. 38 and 39, 174

184. Old Testament, Psalms 8:4, 174

185. Approximate w o r d i n g used by Harold B. Lee, 175

186. Maurice Maeterlinck, *Everybody's Magazine,* July 1911, 176, 177

187. Doctrine and Covenants, 131:7, 177

188. Dr. Harry Emerson Fosdick, *The Intimations of Immortality,* 178

189. Walter Owen, *Sonnet on Death,* No. 87, 179

190. Attributed to John Muir, 179

191. Andrew Jackson, 179

192. Cicero (106 - 43 B.C.), Rom. orator, 180

193. Edward Young, *Night Thoughts,* vii, 180

194. Sir Edwin Arnold, *The New Lucian,* 180

195. Sir William Osler, Farewell Dinner, May 2, 1905, 183

196. James F. Clarke (1810-1888), Am. Unit. Clergyman, 183

197. Farid ud-Din Attar, *Mantik-ut-Tair,* (Fitzgerald tr.), 184

198. Old Testament, Genesis 1:1, 31, 184, 185

199. Bruce Barton, *If a Man Dies, Shall He Live Again?* 185

200. Phillips Brooks, *The Light of the World and Other Sermons: The Seriousness of Life,* 185

201. Alfred Tennyson, *Morte d'Arthur,* 187

202. Mrs. George B. Simmons, "These I Will Keep," *Good Housekeeping,* Jan. 1936, 187

203. Lincoln, Conversation with Maj. Gen. Daniel V. Sickles in a Washington hospital, 187

204. Ibid., Interview with Rev. J. T. Duryea and the Christian Commission, 1865, 187

205. Ibid., J. G. Holland's statement in Life of Abraham Lincoln, 187

206. Ibid., Conversation with Senator James F. Wilson, 188

207. Ibid., To a group of friends, 1862, reported by Dr. Byron Sutherland, 188

208. Ibid., Interview with Mrs. Eliza P. Gurney, 188

209. Ibid., To neighbors and friends on the occasion of his leaving Springfield for Washington. *Lincoln Finds God,* by Ralph G. Lindstrom, 188

210. Confucius, 194

211. Bonell Thornton (1724-68), Eng. humorist, 194

212. Henry Ward Beecher (1813-87), Am. clergy, 195, 207

213. Matthew Prior, *Alma,* 195

214. Dr. David Starr Jordan, *The Call of the Twentieth Century,* 196

215. Doctrine and Covenants, 58:27, 197

216. Phillips Brooks, *New Starts in Life,* 198

217. Carlyle, *Lectures on Heroes,* Lecture II, 198

218. *Capsuled Comments,* September 1969: "Try One Inning," 199

219. Victor Hugo (1802-85), Fr. auth., 200

220. Longfellow, *The Song of Hiawatha,* Pt. 1, 203

221. The Royal Bank of Canada Monthly Letter, Vol. 49 No. 11, 203

222. Old Testament, Malachi 4:6, 204

223. Doctrine and Covenants 38:27, 204

224. Accredited to William James, 207

225. Thomas Bracken, *Not Understood,* 214